PRAISE FOR MESSAGES FROM THE GOLDEN ANGELS

God is in the Little Things: Messages from the Golden Angels exposes the illusion of the physical world's darkness of fear with the brilliance of spiritual light. It reveals the key to experiencing our version of heaven on earth: ascending our energetic vibration to that of love by facing and healing the pain of the past.

This is not just one woman's story. It's my story and it's your story—a story of ascension in human words supported by the energy of love. It's a revelation that when we tap into our inner wisdom and muster our strength from deep within, we can heal the fear that has held us hostage for lifetimes.

Are you ready to expand into the light of your spiritual essence? Patricia's message will support your ability to do it, even though you may be afraid. Her path will validate that yes, your experiences are real! If you're actively ascending and expanding your conscious awareness, Patricia's message will nourish you with renewed resilience! I highly recommend Messages from the Golden Angels.

~Kate Large, best-selling author, founder of Soul Kisses Spiritual Whispers and The Game of Life Mastery

Patricia Brooks is that rare combination of spiritual leader and gripping storyteller. *Messages from the Golden Angels* documents her quest of inner transformation, and as one chapter follows another, she takes the reader

by the hand and continually guides them one step higher on the ladder of awakening to one's true identity. What makes the tale unique is that, while never holding back on deeply personal details of her emotional struggles, she never seems to be talking about herself but instead is always gifting us with a model of how a seeker is led on an ever-expanding path of Divine possibilities. We vicariously live the journey with her and arrive at the end of the book feeling renewed, inspired, and blessed.

~Jeffrey Chappell, international best-selling author of *Answers from Silence*

Patricia Brooks has once again opened her heart and life to us by continuing to share her inspiring healing journey. She willingly shares her agonies as well as her triumphs, powerful ways of communicating with the Divine, and the everyday healing that is available to us if we are only willing to participate. Her openness and insight in sharing her experiences with us is surely a gift of healing that she offers to others.

~Kamala Snow, OUnI interspiritual counselor/minister, soul coach, and teacher

God is in the Little Things: Messages from the Golden Angels conveys a high energy of truth. I was easily able to connect with many points that Patricia raises via her experiences with encountering her golden angels. While reading this book, it was clear that beginning her path of spiritual awakening was scary, as it is for many. I also encountered this on my path while discovering my gift of channeling. I learned, like Patricia, that you must find the courage in yourself to conquer your obstacles and keep your head high—because following your heart will lead to beautiful experiences. I highly recommend this book to anyone wanting to discover more about their own spiritual path.

~Matthew Douglas, channel for the spiritual advisors of Rainbow Walker, author of *The Beginning*, co-founder of Rainbow Walker Books

When I first read *God is in the Little Things: Messages from the Golden Angels*, I savored each passage as one would savor a fine wine. As Patricia Brooks shares this fascinating and very intimate part of her path, we can all relate well to the emerging of the self through the guidance of our own angels. As a gifted writer, she keeps the reader anticipating the next part of her journey, which goes from the painful rejection and heartbreak felt in her divorce to finding herself in a dance, the dance of life. Step by step, she carefully carries the reader in search of their own meaning of the dance.

~Dr. Jean Logan, international best-selling author of Unlocking the Power of Glyphs

God is in the Little Things: Messages from the Golden Angels is an emotionally raw and beautifully-expressed description of Patricia's personal journey of healing deep-seated emotional issues with the glorious guidance of Divine beings that she experienced as golden angels. Through her journey, one can reflect on one's own personal journey of healing. As Patricia healed, she discovered her own angelic self and how valuable we all are to the Divine order, to the Oneness of the universe. This book will enrich your life and help you to recognize that Divine beings are always available to each and every one of us as long as we are open to their unlimited love and support.

~Marie Marchesseault, traditional Usui and Rainbow-Reiki master teacher

God is in the Little Things: Messages from the Golden Angels is absolutely delightful! Patricia Brooks's approach to teaching and sharing her firsthand experiences of awakening and connecting with unseen realms is at once both captivating and alluring while still conveying a childlike innocence that ultimately richly rewards the reader. This book is a true gift to anyone looking to live the life they truly desire.

~Lori Ann Spagna, best-selling author, speaker, luminary, and visionary

Very timely book. ... We are all on a journey of self-awareness and belonging, and I believe that when the student is ready, the teacher appears! Messages from the Golden Angels is definitely the teacher! Thank you, Patricia Brooks, for sharing your story with us, the willing students!

~Carole Matthews, intuitive and radio host

Patricia writes in an honest and open fashion about her emotional and spiritual life in a way that even those who are not on the path can relate with. Her books are not only for those who have not yet begun their spiritual journey but are for seasoned seekers as well. Her healings, readings, and regressions help to open even more channels of communication with her guides as she heals her inner self. This book gives us hope that we can each find our own golden angels and learn to listen to our Higher Self, even in the midst of the human experiences of pain and despair.

~Maria C. Castillo, L.C.S.W, psychotherapist and hypnotherapist, is a contributing author in Miracles Happen: The Transformational Healing Power of Past-Life Memories by Brian L. Weiss, M.D. and Amy Weiss, M.S.W

The reader is sure to be intrigued and inspired as Rev. Patricia Brooks shares, with great warmth and openness, her journey of connecting to the golden beings. Patricia's personal story will lead the reader to appreciate the guidance shared by these angelic beings and remind us that, with an open heart, we too may encounter such experiences. The author opens our eyes to a remarkable world of light and love. What a gift!

~Rev. Lynette Turner, Positivoligist™

GOD IS IN THE LITTLE THINGS

MESSAGES FROM THE GOLDEN ANGELS

Books by Patricia Brooks

*God is in the Little Things:
Messages from the Animals*

*God is in the Little Things:
Messages from the Golden Angels*

www.revpatriciabrooks.com

GOD IS IN THE *Little Things*

MESSAGES FROM THE GOLDEN ANGELS

PATRICIA BROOKS

MY JOURNEY CONTINUES

Copyright © 2016

All rights reserved.

This book or part thereof may not be reproduced in any form, stored in a retrieval system, or transmitted in any form by any means-electronic, mechanical, photocopy, recording, or otherwise without prior written permission of the publisher, except as provided by United States of America copyright law.

The information provided in this book is designed to provide helpful information on the subjects discussed. This book is not meant to be used, nor should it be used, to diagnose or treat any medical condition. The author and publisher are not responsible for any specific health needs that may require medical supervision and are not liable for any damages or negative consequences from any treatment, action, application, or preparation, to any person reading or following the information in this book.

References are provided for information purposes only and do not constitute endorsement of any websites or other sources. In the event you use any of the information in this book for yourself, the author and the publisher assume no responsibility for your actions.

Books may be purchased through booksellers or by contacting Sacred Stories Publishing.

God is in the Little Things: Messages from the Golden Angels
Patricia Brooks
Tradepaper ISBN: 978-1-945026-00-3
Electronic ISBN: 978-1-945026-01-0

Library of Congress Control Number: 2016903846

Published by Sacred Stories Publishing
Delray Beach, FL
www.sacredstoriespublishing.com

Printed in the United States of America

ACKNOWLEDGMENTS

To my daughters Lindsey and Megan: thank you for always believing in me and encouraging me, even during the times when it was more than what you could see or what you could touch. I love you. #TeamBrooks always

To my dear friend Kathleen: my story could not have been written without your love and your phenomenal coaching skills. With your help, my story has come to life.

To my amazing editor Chryse Wymer: your heart, humor and exceptional understanding of the English language has shaped my story into an engaging read.

To my soul friends who are walking my path with me: thank you for your friendship, your love and your Light. We are on an incredible journey.

To the Lightworkers and Wayshowers I have not yet met: thank you for holding a Higher Consciousness for all of us.

And finally to my golden angels: words fall short in expressing my love and my gratitude for your presence in my life.

MESSAGES FROM THE GOLDEN ANGELS

is dedicated to my parents Vito and Grace Cagganello.

Dad, even when the days were long and your pain unbearable, you never wavered in your faith. You found joy in the little things and offered your pain to your Lord. It is in those moments that you found your peace, and by watching you, I found my faith.

Mom, even when your body was exhausted, your heart broken, and I thought you couldn't continue on, you drew your strength from your angels, and somehow, you did. It is in those moments that you showed what love really is, and by watching you, I found my strength.

"THE DANCE"

I have sent you my invitation,
the note inscribed on the palm of my hand by the fire of living.
Don't jump up and shout, "Yes, this is what I want! Let's do it!"
Just stand up quietly and dance with me.

Show me how you follow your deepest desires,
spiraling down into the ache within the ache,
and I will show you how I reach inward and open outward
to feel the kiss of the Mystery, sweet lips on my own, every day.

Don't tell me you want to hold the whole world in your heart.
Show me how you turn away from making another wrong without
abandoning yourself when
you are hurt and afraid of being unloved.

Tell me a story of who you are,
and see who I am in the stories I am living.
And together we will remember that each of us
always has a choice.

Don't tell me how wonderful things will be . . . some day.
Show me you can risk being completely at peace,
truly okay with the way things are right now in this moment,
and again in the next and the next and the next. . . .

I have heard enough warrior stories of heroic daring.
Tell me how you crumble when you hit the wall,
the place you cannot go beyond by the strength of your own will.
What carries you to the other side of that wall,
to the fragile beauty of your own humanness?

And after we have shown each other how we have set and
kept the clear, healthy boundaries
that help us live side by side with each other,
let us risk remembering that we never stop
silently loving those we once loved out loud.

Take me to the places on the earth that teach you how to dance,
the places where you can risk letting the world break your heart.
And I will take you to the places where the earth
beneath my feet and the stars overhead make
my heart whole again and again.

Show me how you take care of business
without letting business determine who you are.
When the children are fed but still the voices within and around us
shout that soul's desires have too high a price,
let us remind each other that it is never about the money.

Show me how you offer to your people and the world
the stories and the songs you want our
children's children to remember.
And I will show you how I struggle not to change the world,
but to love it.

Sit beside me in long moments of shared solitude,
knowing both our absolute aloneness and
our undeniable belonging.
Dance with me in the silence and in the sound of small daily words,
holding neither against me at the end of the day.

And when the sound of all the declarations of our
sincerest intentions has died away on the wind,
dance with me in the infinite pause before the next great inhale
of the breath that is breathing us all into being,
not filling the emptiness from the outside or from within.

Don't say, "Yes!"
Just take my hand and dance with me.

Used with permission from Oriah Mountain Dreamer, The Dance © 2001. Published by HarperOne. All rights reserved. www.oriah.org

FOREWORD

These are very special times for our planet and humanity, as we are destined to ascend into higher frequencies of existence through raising our consciousness. This is all taking place once again through the support and love from higher realms. We are embracing our multi-dimensionality by directly connecting to the forces from whence we came. This is our divine destiny.

In effect, we are all in the process of activating our soul plans (our reason to be here) by knowing who we are, why we are here, and how to apply our talents and gifts into world service. Since we are all unique individuals, and the universe would be incomplete without each of us here, we all have a story, or stories, to tell that support the evolution of our *selves* and the world.

As someone who has had many connections with higher realms and written many books about that connection, I find this a fascinating, fulfilling, personal journey like no other.

We are not alone—we never have been and never will be; our guides and guardians (call them what you will) are forever beside us. *God is in the Little Things:*

Messages from the Golden Angels is a major reminder of this truth; through a personal, almost diary like, story, we are reconnected with the higher realms (energies/forces/golden angels) empowering us, awakening our individual life plan. We feel the main character's feelings, her doubts and fears and eventual enlightenment, as an essential aspect of her feminine energy. We become her, and One.

Through this personal journey, we are reassured that we are never alone and that there are golden angels all around to love and support us until we can learn how to completely love ourselves the way they love us. That is their mission, and ours.

I shall not reveal all the lovely details in this book; they are yours to discover and savor and know within you.

Through revealing her heart and soul, our heroine reflects/mirrors our own hearts and souls. We are surrendering to not knowing in order to know. This cosmic choreography becomes our divine dance as well. A daring dance unique to the book's central character becomes ours . . . We are merging and morphing into Oneness.

~Phillip Elton Collins, co-founder of The Angel News Network

PREFACE

Let me introduce you to my golden angels. They are my messengers and my guides. But even more so, they are my friends. How do I explain them to you? Convey the magnificence of beings that are so loving, so wondrous, that they are beyond description?

I believe I will just tell you about them.

CHAPTER 1

"C'mon, c'mon, they're here!" Kate shouted to us as she straightened her long black wig and hat once again.

"I'm coming!" I replied, yelling over the racket of the busy restaurant kitchen. "Give me one sec; I just have to drop this order off at table eight."

"Meet us at table fourteen when you're ready." Kate tossed the words over her shoulder as she hurried forward.

I smiled and watched as a black cat, a French maid, and a sexy witch, my friends and fellow waitresses, made their way over to table fourteen. "I can't wait to meet him . . . He is supposed to be so nice . . . and really cute . . ." I could hear Kate exclaim to our friends as they rushed off.

Saturday night was always busy at the restaurant, and tonight, being Halloween, it was even busier. The restaurant was filled with elaborately-dressed ghouls and goblins enjoying a quick dinner before heading out to a Halloween party of their own.

I dropped my order off at table eight dressed as Peter Pan—complete with my green pointed booties and a feather in my cap—and went to meet Kate's daughter and her date for the evening. Kate had been talking about this all week. Her daughter, Tina, worked with this guy at another restaurant in town, and she had been hoping he would ask her out for a while. They were stopping in for a bite to eat and to say hello before they, too, went out for the evening.

"Hi! I'm Peter . . . I mean, Patty," I jokingly blurted as I arrived at table fourteen.

"Great, you're here! Yes, let me introduce you. Well, you already know Tina, and this is her date, Steve," Kate offered.

"Hi, Tina. It's great to see you again," I warmly greeted her. Tina, my friend Kate's daughter, was a sweet girl with long straight blond hair and a quick smile on her pretty face. Tina wasn't much younger than me, but working with and being friends with her mom made me feel much older.

"Nice to meet you." I turned to Steve, her date, and extended my hand to shake his.

"Nice to meet you too," he replied.

Our hands clasped, and our eyes met, and I found myself staring into eyes that I already knew—eyes that I had known forever. An electric jolt went through my body. It was so intense that I wondered if he felt too. This person, Steve, was someone important to me. I wasn't sure how or what was going to happen next, but I knew we were meant to be together. I was sure of it.

It has been almost twenty-five years since that first Halloween. I was a twenty-eight-year-old former marine, full-time student, and part-time waitress then, and I had met who I believed to be the man of my dreams: Steve, a cute long-haired part-time cook, part-time construction worker, and part-time guitarist in a metal band.

We were opposites in almost every way. A former sergeant in the U.S. Marine Corps and a young adult in my late twenties, I lived with my parents, determined to pay for and finish my college education; Steve, a few years younger, lived with two friends in a bachelor-style house and enjoyed the party lifestyle of the area. I was a planner; Steve went with the flow. I, an intellectual, enjoyed books and learning; Steve was masterful with his hands, whether in his job as a trim carpenter or refinishing his father's prized guitar. Steve was musical, singing and playing guitar in a local metal band, while I was only comfortable singing in the car alone with the windows rolled up.

Steve didn't feel the jolt that first Halloween night, but I never forgot it. Despite our differences—and just as I knew in my heart that we would—we began to build our life together. One thing we did share was a love of discussing deep, almost esoteric, topics, whether spiritual or secular in nature. We were young adults trying to understand our place in the cosmos, and my religious upbringing as a Roman Catholic and Steve's upbringing as a Southern Baptist only added to the richness of our discourse.

As I reflected back, a single mom of two beautiful daughters, I have realized that was what we lost in the busyness of life: we lost our love to discuss, debate, share, and wonder aloud at the mysteries of the universe and the intricacies of our very souls.

Nowhere in my life plans did I envision myself being rejected and alone at fifty-years old—to have to start over at the point in my life that it should have been easier. To lose, despite all of our differences, the person I believed to be my soul mate. But I was—rejected, that is—and it hit me hard. It knocked me to my knees.

Life is funny that way, I guess. It changes. Life changes the rules, and it changes you. Despite our best efforts to keep it the same, and most times without much warning, life changes.

My life, and a large part of my identity, was forever changed when Steve left. I have been divorced for a little over three years now, and I have spent the majority of that time trying to pick myself up and figure out who I really am. With a lot of frustration, tears, anger, gratitude, and love, I am getting there.

What I eventually realized is that when I got divorced, I lost my identity as part of a couple, a wife—the Mrs. I was to my kids' friends and our larger community. But I had really lost—or more correctly, *forgotten*—my real identity a long, long time ago.

CHAPTER 2

"You are in a depression," a voice quietly whispered in my ear and interrupted my thoughts.

I whirled my head around to find an older woman, possibly in her sixties, looking at me through deep-brown eyes filled with understanding and compassion. Nicely dressed in light-green slacks and a matching jacket the color of the newborn spring when the leaves are unspoiled and fresh, she hesitatingly smiled.

"I didn't mean to disturb you," she went on to say, "but your angels asked me to tell you that you are in a depression and need to get help."

In the noisy din of the coffeehouse, my hand shook as I put my coffee cup down. "What did you say?" I asked, feeling confused, jarred from my thoughts by her presence and her words.

She laid her perfectly-manicured hand on my shoulder, and like a person consoling a frightened child, she gave it a comforting rub. The vibrant red of her fingernails, and the many rings that adorned her fingers, distracted me for a moment—until she spoke again.

"Your angels asked me to tell you that the volume is so loud around you that it brings discouragement. You must be quiet. Quiet your mind, and ask God and the angels to help you heal."

I couldn't reply; my throat instantly tightened upon hearing her words. I nodded my head and closed my eyes, squeezed them shut, trying to stop the tears that had welled up inside of them.

Could she be right? Was I in a depression? I cried a lot—every day, in fact. I argued with my kids and isolated myself from my family and friends. It was easier that way. I didn't have to talk about how I felt or look into their eyes and see their concern or pity. How was I supposed to explain my feelings anyway? They ran the gamut from sadness to fear to anger to feeling overwhelmed, and sometimes even to feeling relief. It had only been a few months since Steve had left. *How else was I supposed to feel?*

In my heart, I knew the angels' words rang true. But it was more than that. I felt like I was drowning. My chest pounded, and my throat constricted from the emotional pain. Any effort to try to stop the tears from falling only caused them to explode out of me in deep and painful sobs.

I needed help. Spiritual help from God and from my angels. They were right: I knew I couldn't do it alone. I had lost a part of myself, of my heart, during the divorce, and I needed to find a way to reclaim it.

Deep in my soul, I knew that my religious understanding of who I was and why things happened were no longer enough for me. My heart and my mind both pleaded with me to become whole again. My soul was asking me to look for more, to go deeper, and to find the answers, the meaning to my struggles.

I began to seek out people and experiences and teachings that were more spiritual in nature than what I was familiar with. I learned about auras and chakras and ways to balance and heal our energetic fields. I connected with the energies of the earth, and I was being introduced to animal totems. These teachings were not meant to replace my religious foundation but to deepen my connection to and understanding of it, and me.

During this soul searching, I heard about an open house for a new interfaith church in my community. In an interfaith community, all religions and spiritual practices are honored and respected. The belief is that there are many paths to the mountaintop, many ways to remember your spiritual Truth. Our Truth, the Divine essence we share, is the same, but the way we can connect to it is varied.

I was intrigued and wanted to know more. Early one Saturday afternoon, I took a fateful drive to the place that would become my spiritual home. Entering the newly-refurbished building, I had a sense of anticipation that I had not felt for a long while, and standing on the threshold, I paused and breathed—deep breaths to center my thoughts and calm my beating heart. Immediately, I was struck by the painting across from me. Delicate white blossoms on the tips of almond branches gently hung against the bluest of skies, and I recognized it as the same painting that adorned the cover of my new journal. Smiling, I walked forward.

A serene energy permeated the space and welcomed me as I stepped into the sanctuary. Vanilla-scented candles mixed with the faintest fragrance cast from abundant bouquets of white lilies. Soft instrumental music played as a soothing backdrop, and tiny white lights, strung across the ceiling, cast a soft glow. Religious symbols from many different faiths adorned the walls: The Christian cross, the Jewish Star of David, the Islamic Star and Crescent, the Hindu Om, the Tao Yin and Yang, and the Buddhist Triple Treasure were present and welcomed all people and all beliefs.

People were milling about and making new friends. A tall woman with short dark-brown hair and a ready laugh caught my attention. Wearing a white robe with a purple stole that draped across her shoulders and fell just below her hips, she was warmly welcoming everyone. Soon, she came up to me.

"Welcome! I am Reverend Chris, and I am happy that you are here," she said in greeting as she clasped my hands in a warm embrace.

"Thank you. I'm happy to be here," I softly replied, suddenly shy in her presence.

Reverend Chris looked at me quizzically. I wondered if she found it odd that I was shy, until she next spoke.

"Do I know you?" she questioned, her gaze now penetrating. "You seem so familiar to me."

I understood what she felt. I felt it too. "No, we have never met," I replied, realizing that my sudden shyness was due to the huge rush of energy I felt from her.

"Hmm, we must be soul sisters," she said with a twinkle in her eyes.

"Yes, I believe we must be."

CHAPTER 3

Attending services regularly, I made many new friends, spiritual seekers like myself. Our community was filled with people of all ages, ethnicities, sexual orientations, interests, and varied foundational religious beliefs. The more different we were, the more we found that we were the same. Acceptance, tolerance, and love are basic tenets of interfaith spirituality, and we saw and honored in each other our common bond: our Divine Spirit.

One of the many blessings that came to me as a member of this community was meeting a woman named Lynette Turner. Lynette had, among many other gifts, the gift to communicate with the angels. She described it as walking with one foot in the physical realm and one foot in the spiritual realm. The angels spoke to her, and through her, in sessions called angel readings. Lynette lovingly and generously shared her gift with others.

When I found out that Lynette could hear the angels speak, I knew that I needed to have a session with her. I was seeking guidance and a deeper understanding of myself, a way to heal. To have the angels speak to me and give me guidance through Lynette would be a remarkable opportunity, I thought. I scheduled a session for Lynette's first availability, an evening appointment in the upcoming week.

Sessions with Lynette were two-hours long, during which time she would listen to the guidance the angels were conveying to her and then relay the messages to you. Lynette explained that while she was fully conscious, and not in a trance-like state, she would not remember what was said after the session. She encouraged me to take notes during the session, as there would be too much information to remember it all. Notes were also encouraged because what might seem unimportant or irrelevant at the time could, upon further reflection or at a later time, have a much deeper meaning for you than you at first realized. In addition to hearing the angels directly, Lynette might also ask you to pull angel cards for more guidance. The cards that you drew were a way for your own Spirit, your Higher Self, to reach out and offer assistance.

I was breathless with anticipation. Ever since my angels spoke through the woman in the coffee shop, I wanted more contact. As a child, my mother would talk about angels and comfort me with stories of my guardian angels watching over me. To this day, her home is filled with statues and pictures of beautiful angels—each one, I believe, watching over me in their special way. The thought that my angels would soon speak to me through Lynette filled me with awe and gratitude. I was optimistic that this would be a turning point for me and that the dark, heavy fog of hopelessness that had been encircling and pervading my thoughts, my moods, and my heart would soon begin to lighten.

The night I had been waiting for finally came, and I drove—perhaps, in my excitement, a little too fast—to the church where Lynette had her office. Arriving a few minutes early, I made myself a cup of tea and happily found myself in a beautiful space overflowing with a peaceful and loving energy. "Angels Gather Here" was inscribed on a plaque that hung above the door, and a gorgeous purple tapestry depicting a group of angels decorated the far wall. Clear crystals and purple amethysts shimmered on the table, scattered among white candles of varying heights.

"Hello, Patty. I am happy to see you!" Lynette exclaimed, rousing me back to the moment.

"Hi, Lynette," I exuberantly replied and reached out to give her a warm hug.

"Ready to begin?" she asked, although I suspect she already knew the answer.

"Yes! No pressure, but I have been waiting all week for tonight!" I smiled and sat down.

Sitting across the table from Lynette, with my journal covered in almond blossoms before me, I took in Lynette's kind brown eyes and cheerful smile. They welcomed and calmed me.

I trusted Lynette implicitly and felt my body begin to relax. This was right, and this was good. The warmth and sense of well-being that spread through my body reassured me. My angels were with me and they were ready to help.

"My angel, named Crystal, is with me, and she is here to make sure that I convey everything in a crystal-clear manner," Lynette began. "She has long blond, wavy hair, and crystals adorn her gown.

"Please feel comfortable to ask any questions that you have, and if you're ready, we'll begin.

"Your first angel tonight is Clarice, a female angel with long, curly, red hair, wearing a multicolored robe filled with blues, greens, and gold strewn through it. Gold and silver rings are on each finger, and long gold-hoop earrings are in her ears. Clarice has a bubbly personality and is happy to be with you tonight," Lynette shared with me.

"Patty, you need to be more playful. Lighten up and feel the joy, even before you figure everything out," Clarice begins to say. "And give more credit to yourself!

"Sing! Sing with me: 'This little light of mine, I'm gonna let it shine. This little light of mine, I'm gonna let it shine. This little light of mine, I'm gonna let it shine, let it shine, let it shine, let it shine!' because Patty, you are to start letting your light shine!" Clarice gaily states.

I am dumbfounded. Did an angel named Clarice just sing a favorite childhood song of mine—to me? Did she tell me to let my light shine?

I have no time to think as Clarice quickly continues, "You have just scratched the surface of your potential. But you must let go of the fear, Patty. Trust the Universe. We will not let you fall. You are not alone.

"Designate contemplation time and think about what makes your heart sing! You have very good instincts and can do spiritual work."

Clarice lovingly goes on to say, "There are no wrong paths, and there are no roadblocks. Whatever you need will come to you, and your spiritual journey will be an abundant one.

"But you must listen to yourself! Not what you think in your head but what you feel in your heart. Don't judge— just trust it, even if it's not logical. Give yourself permission to *think outside the box.*

"You are worthy, Patty. Be grateful, and believe that you are worthy."

Abruptly, Lynette stops speaking and looks perplexed. "A presence has come forward that is not an angel. This usually doesn't happen, and I don't know who he is, but he is a loving presence," she says.

Bewildered, Lynette goes on to say, "He wants me to tell you 'chin up, and shoulders back'."

I smile. Instantly, I know that it is my dad. I am a former U.S. Marine, and my dad was so proud of me. Those words transported me back to the first time he said them to me: my graduation from marine boot camp in Parris Island, S.C. Wrapping me in the first hug in nine long weeks, he stepped back and looked me up and down. "Chin up, and shoulders back, Marine," he said with a smile. As the years went on, even long after I returned to civilian life, my dad would frequently say "chin up, and shoulders back" as his way of showing encouragement and letting me know he had faith in me. With those few simple words, my dad has not only told me he is with me but reassures me that, with a positive attitude and determination, I would be able to get through this.

Feelings of love and gratitude wash over me; I put down my pen and breathe. As my dad leaves, Lynette tells me I have an angel with yellow wings that is with me to help me. When I need a loving presence, she will come and wrap her wings around me, to comfort me.

As I smile at the thought of being embraced by an angel, Ruby, a middle-aged female angel with long brown hair and ruby-red slippers, comes forward to speak.

"Patty, you will be leading a group setting, and you will be storytelling. Your challenges will be examples for others of moving into a brighter place," Ruby explains.

"*Listen to us, your angels. Speak your peace about your spirituality and about your angels,*" Ruby counsels. "*Believe in miracles because you are a miracle. Embrace the little miracles and prepare for bigger ones to come.*"

My hands shake as tingles go up and down my spine. I am worthy! I am a miracle! My challenges will be examples for others of moving into a brighter place! *This is truly incredible but somehow feels so right, so true to me.*

Ruby continues to speak, "*Keep a notebook by your bed, Patty, and write every day. Feel free and playful. A door is opening to a new stage of life, and we will not guide you where you are not supposed to go.*

"*You are to write a book.*"

Wow. The pen rolled unnoticed out of my hand. Thoughts, feelings, and questions swirled around in my head and demanded my attention. My eyes met Lynette's, and she smiled.

"Take some time. You've been given a lot of information to absorb," she suggested. "Read your notes again in a few days, as then they will give you even more insight."

Yes, I definitely needed time to reflect. I was a high-school computer-science teacher and unbeknownst to Lynette, I had just been accepted into a doctoral program for educational leadership. My studies to earn my Ed.D degree were supposed to start the following winter semester.

My angels knew my plans, though, and they seemed to have something very different for me in mind. They told me I should consider holistic or spiritual work and to take note of my journey because I was about to write a book. The thought that I was to make a career change, especially now, after I was experiencing so many other changes in my life, was more than I thought I could handle. To tell me that I would soon write a book ... was incredible. I was a computer-science teacher, not a writer.

CHAPTER 4

You are worthy, Patty. Listen to your heart. I clung to Clarice's advice, the reassurances that I was loved and worthy. That's what I was really looking for: some reassurance that I would soon feel better. Although my hands were sore from writing, my breath quickened, and a lightness began to come into my heart. I knew that I had just received a valuable gift, and I felt a strong, supportive presence around me.

"You are worthy" and "believe in miracles because you are a miracle" renewed my hope in the future and gave me a glimpse of my self-worth—something I hadn't felt in a long time.

"Feel the joy even before you figure it out," Clarice had said. I had a lot of work to do in order to reclaim a sense of joy and peace in my life, and now that I was given some direction and guidance, I was going to follow it. Thankfully, it was the beginning of summer, and as a teacher on break from school, I was fortunate to have the time to focus on me.

At the time, pursuing spiritual work didn't resonate with me; however, the angels had also suggested something else, something that took my breath away. The angels encouraged me to dance more. Reconnect with my soul through the joy of music. I "moved like a pretty little bird," Ruby had said, and she strongly suggested I attend a dance workshop at a retreat center in a neighboring state. She also told me to get rid of my fear of dancing. "Lose your ego and enjoy yourself," Ruby had stressed.

This was unbelievable. Of all the things the angels were telling me, I couldn't believe that they were telling me to dance. Dance to reconnect with my soul and to find my joy. Many times in my life, I had wished that I could feel the joy I saw on others people's faces while I watched them dance—looks of pure abandon and bliss, as if the music moved through them and became their very lifeblood, nourishing their heart and soul.

I yearned to feel that freedom, but one unforgettable night, deep scars were burned indelibly into my teenage psyche. As frenetic flashes of color from the strobe lights cut across the dance floor and the deafening reverberation of the bass pounded in my ears, I whirled around and was confronted with a pointed finger and merciless cackles from a nearby group of girls. Under the pulsating disco ball, I was left exposed and vulnerable. Even though the hustle was finally not the only dance in town, my feelings of awkwardness and inadequacy lingered.

My angels knew this. Ruby had told me that "when you get up the courage to dance, you can use that new sense of self-worth and take it into other aspects of your life." It sounded plausible. But they wanted me to dance! This was huge for me. But I had felt so bad for so long, and the promise of feeling joy tantalized my every sense. I was willing to try almost anything to feel better—even if it meant getting up the courage to dance in front of others.

I checked out the Web site of a nearby retreat center, half hoping they wouldn't offer anything for me. Sure enough, right under the site's bright-green banner, a special event was listed: a two-day workshop that used dance as a way to express and connect more deeply to your inner self. I sat there for a long time, staring at the computer screen, unsure what to do. I knew this was a defining moment for me. The angels had told me something very specific to do. If I believed in their guidance, then I needed to be serious about following it. What would I choose: find the audacity to face my own "not good enough" feelings head-on, hoping I would soon feel better, or stay in this safe, but sad, shell that I had built around myself, regardless of how miserable I felt? My decision, I knew, had been made when I had turned on the computer. I signed up for the workshop that day.

Quickly, doubt didn't just creep in; it poured in. I frantically pushed it back, knowing that I only needed one tiny reason not to go. And I did not want to find it.

What are you thinking? The workshop is next week. How are you ever going to make arrangements for your kids, your pets, and your house by next week? and more pointedly, Why would you ever go to a dance workshop anyway? You can't dance! My ego and my Spirit locked horns, my head and my heart being mercilessly batted back and forth.

But as all of my arrangements for my responsibilities—my kids, my pets, and my house—were effortlessly made, I knew in my heart that I was meant to go. The day soon arrived, and I packed my bags with yoga pants, T-shirts, headbands, and threw in a touch of resiliency and self-deprecation for good measure. I kissed my girls good-bye, tossed my bags in the back of my old, gray Nissan, and as I settled comfortably in my seat, a strange tingling ran down my spine.

Could this be the beginning of positive feelings starting to return to my body?

The retreat center, a large series of brick buildings nestled protectively in the bosom of a nearby mountain range, was a two-hour drive away. Driving through the rolling New England countryside, the time passed quickly. "Get the Party Started," a rocking song from my favorite artist, Pink, blasted from the stereo. On repeat, the rhythmic sounds and upbeat lyrics helped loosen my inhibitions as I drummed my fingers on the steering wheel and twisted to the beat. As the sun was nearing its highest point, my car crested a hill, and while a vista of trees and gently-sloping hills greeted me, I came upon my home for the next two days.

A sense of community greeted me as I drove down the long, winding driveway. The energy in the air shifted, as if feelings of peace and contentment were infused into the space. Time seemed to slow, and I noticed little things: the clanging of the screen door as it closed loudly behind a guest, a lone dandelion missed by the gardener in the neatly-tended flower garden, and a beautiful canopy of trees shading a wooden bench that beckoned me to sit and rest. People walked out of the woods, hiking boots on and water bottles in hand, and I made a mental note to find out about the hiking trails on the property.

My emotions fluctuated between "what the heck am I doing here?" and "I never want to leave!" My father's words "chin up, and shoulders back" came to mind. His words brought a smile to my lips and tenacity to my heart, and I parked my car, grabbed my bags, and I walked into the foyer to sign in.

Thirsty from my drive, I was delighted to see that a large carafe of fruit-infused water had been put out to welcome guests. After two large cups of strawberry-lemon water, I was refreshed by the tangy sweetness and ready to start. I signed in, dropped my bags in my room, and followed the directions down to the workshop.

My newfound sense of confidence, however, quickly abated as I walked up to the workshop door and was greeted by a white shoe rack. A six-foot wide, three-level piece of wood, designed to hold shoes, stopped me cold. Sneakers, sandals, and ballet flats in all sizes—some small enough to fit a tiny woman's feet, others large enough for a very tall man's, and in shades from white to black and all colors in between—were there on that rack. But these were not just random shoes to me. My breath caught as I realized that these were the shoes of the people I was going to have to dance with!

Who are these people? I bet most of them are great dancers ... especially whoever has these pretty red shoes. My fears taunted me once again. *Could they be nervous like me?* I halfheartedly hoped, feeling intimately connected to the owners of the anonymous shoes left on this rack. I looked down at my size ten, worn-out black flip-flops and sighed. I hesitantly placed mine on the rack with theirs, berated myself for not wearing nicer shoes, said a quick prayer, and entered the room.

The large rectangular room was lined on two sides with tall windows, rounded at the top, which allowed sunlight to stream onto the glistening hardwood floor, casting comforting warmth into the room. As my mind noted the room's beautiful characteristics, my heart knew I was really entering a room filled with possibilities: a breakthrough, a fresh start, and a new perspective were all whispers on the winds of promise here.

The room was filled with expectant and smiling people sitting on the hardwood floor, waiting to begin. My mind quickly estimated that there had to be at least a hundred people here, but I especially noted a group of three women sitting together, casually chatting. They seemed to be about my age, and I wondered if they were friends who came together or if they had only just met. *Maybe one of them wore the pretty red shoes on the rack outside* . . . I thought, feeling self-conscious that I didn't have anyone to talk to, and my confidence faltered again. Against a wall in the back of the room, I sat down and tried to assess the situation. As I glanced at the door, I gratefully realized that the place I chose to sit also gave me an easy escape if I changed my mind.

Before I could flee, a young woman stepped up to the front of the room. Dressed in black yoga pants and a white tank top, she looked to be in her late twenties. As she tossed back her long brown hair, she threw her arms wide and welcomed us with a big smile on her face. I anxiously thought back to what my angels told me during my reading: "We will not lead you somewhere you are not supposed to go." I made a conscious choice to stay and trust them.

"We are going to jump right in," Deborah, our instructor, said, her warmth and exuberance comforting me. "Since this is expressive dance, there is no right or wrong way. Simply let the music wash over you, caressing each part of you, and move your beautiful body in response in whatever way feels good to you."

Slow instrumental music that I had never heard before filled the room, and we collectively stood, taking cues from each other, and began to dance. At first, we danced individually, and I lost myself, a wounded bird trying out her wings. I moved nervously on the outskirts of this large mass of people moving and swaying their bodies to the music.

It wasn't so bad. If I closed my eyes, which I did frequently at first, I did feel the music. I would raise my arms above my head, and the music would flow into my fingertips, down my body, and into my very core as the soft melodies caressed my hurt and broken heart. We danced this way for some time; the music would change, but with my eyes closed, I was still the wounded bird on the outskirts, trying out her wings. Occasionally, I snuck a peek at the others, to make sure I didn't look too different, and eventually, I started to feel safe, secure that I could survive this workshop.

But then the rules changed. They wouldn't allow me to simply close my eyes and retreat into myself, dancing amongst—but really at a distance from—the others. We were now asked to dance through the crowd, stop briefly at different people, and dance with them for a moment or two before we moved on to someone else.

I had to make eye contact—seek out others and dance with them. Expose, even for the briefest of moments, the part of myself that I didn't feel confident in . . . and never had. *If I look into their eyes, would I see the same mean laughter I saw all those years ago under the pulsating disco ball? Would I feel the same humiliation?*

I glanced back at the large door I had walked through just a few short hours before—the escape I had tucked neatly into my back pocket. Two choices lay before me. One, I could walk out that door, out of the room, and not do it. Not put myself and my wounded heart out there. I could simply leave. That choice actually scared me more than the dancing. I knew that if I did that, then I would be stuck, stuck in this horrible "not good enough" feeling that I had been living with. The other choice was to dance, not with my eyes closed in my own safe, secure world but with others. The little self-worth I had left from my divorce was not going to be enough to get me through this. I thought of my angels, felt them—a beautiful collective of light just above me—and asked for their help.

You told me to do this, I reminded them. Please be with me now.

My breath quieted my beating heart, and I moved through the crowd. Clumsy at first, I didn't make direct eye contact with the first few people, staring instead just above their eyes and dancing quickly away from them, not allowing them to see me through my eyes—the doorway into my soul.

The other people around me were smiling, laughing even; they were enjoying this. I forced a smile onto my face, determined to feel some of the joy that I had witnessed in the room—even if I had to fake it. As I began to smile at my partners, they smiled back. We connected first through our eyes, and then with each new person, I connected a little more through the movement of our bodies. I slowly became part of this vibrant sea of swaying people; my smile became less forced, coming more from my heart and less from my mind.

Eventually, the music stopped. The first day was over, and I was glad, relieved really, but less relieved than I thought was possible. People hugged around me, seemingly happy for the closeness that this exercise brought to our group. We naturally drifted in groups toward the door, to collect our shoes and head on to dinner. I grinned inwardly as a short red-headed woman in my group put on the pretty red shoes that I had noticed that morning. Her name was Cheryl, and with a ready smile creating fine laugh lines around her mouth and a sparkle in her green eyes, those shoes fit her perfectly.

Dinner was delicious, and the conversation with my group was light and engaging. We shared our stories: where we lived, family, kids, and jobs—just enough to create a bond but not too much to give away who we really were. After dinner, I attended a Buddhist meditation that soothed and uplifted my heart. Physically, emotionally, and spiritually tired from the day, I went to bed and woke early, refreshed and ready for what the day would bring.

The morning dance passed pleasantly. I could now look into the eyes of my partners and truly smile back at them. I even found myself picking up a brightly-colored scarf, provided to us as props, twirling it as I danced. *Who am I?* I laughed to myself.

However, nearing the end of the workshop, I learned that my newfound sense of ease was going to be tested again.

With a smile wider than I thought possible, Deborah explained that she had something very special in store for us. During the next part of the workshop, we were not going to dance with a partner but *for* a partner.

What? My mind raced. *Did she say for a partner? Dance while someone was specifically watching me?*

"I would like everyone to find a partner," she mercilessly went on. "You will each take turns dancing alone. The role of the partner is to simply *watch* you dance."

I froze. This was too much. Even with the increased confidence I had felt in the past two days, this was more than I was ready to handle. This wasn't pushing my limits; this was knocking them down and trampling on them as I raced past. I thought of the door, my escape. Was now the time to pull it out of my back pocket and run like hell?

People were talking, looking for someone to partner with. I hesitantly lifted my eyes and found another set of eyes staring straight into mine. I recognized the sparkle, the green. Cheryl smiled, and I smiled back; I had somehow just silently agreed to be her partner.

You move like a pretty little bird, Patty, my angels again reminded me.

Please stay with me! I pleaded to my angels. *Help me to feel the music, to become the music. Allow me to experience the joy of the music not only in my body but in my soul.*

In that moment, I realized that this is what it was really about: feeling the joy. To reclaim that part of myself, that connection, I had denied for so long. My angels knew that allowing me the freedom to dance would allow me the freedom to reconnect to that lost part of myself.

I took a few deep breaths, gave a final plea to my angels, and stepped onto the dance floor. I was hesitant at first but only for a moment; determination had filled my veins. The importance of this moment was not lost on me, and I wasn't prepared to let it slip by.

You move like a pretty little bird, my angels said again.

And I did. I danced. I swayed. I swirled around and around. I gratefully felt the music caress me, and as I reached my arms up to the angels, I felt their warm embrace. I knew my angels were with me, and I smiled.

When the music ended, I was disappointed because I wanted to dance more. My eyes met Cheryl's as I walked off the floor.

"I truly enjoyed watching you dance," she shared. "Are you a professional dancer?"

I laughed and shook my head. "No, I'm not a professional dancer," I assured her. "But I really did enjoy dancing just then."

The workshop ended; my heart fuller, my mood lighter, and with contentment now also packed in my bags, I drove home. Somehow, two days of dancing had shifted something inside of me. But it wasn't just dancing; my Spirit knew it was so much more. It was two days of finding the confidence to step out into a sea of people and dance. Two days of release, release of my self-limiting beliefs and a constraining sense of self. Two days of trust, trust that I could allow myself to reconnect with my inner self and know I was safe and supported. And finally, two days of joy, the kind of joy that you feel when you surrender all of your defenses and realize that you are loved and you are worthy. Loved not for *what* you are, or for *who* you are, but simply *because you are*.

CHAPTER 5

My experience at the dance workshop was transformative. I had felt joy! Being unable to sustain that joy didn't worry me. I remembered how the feeling started in the depths of my stomach and spread outward, permeating every cell of my body as my lungs were forced to take in more air. As I inhaled deeply, my skin felt prickly as my body took on a heightened sensitivity. As my heart expanded within my chest, my lips could not help but turn upward in a grin. Yes, I remembered what joy felt like.

I didn't know at the time what my spiritual journey was supposed to look like, but I knew that it would be a joyful one. That was all the motivation I needed to keep trusting and walking down my spiritual path.

I was open to new possibilities and experiences, so when Michael, a member of my interfaith church, mentioned that in September, a new session would begin for the interfaith seminary school that our ministers had attended, I was intrigued. It was a two-year program that culminated with ordination as an interfaith minister. As part of the program, I would study many of the world's religions and religious practices. Since I was still unclear as to the direction of my spiritual path, I decided the best thing I could do was study. As I engrossed myself in great spiritual teachings, the wisdom of the ages, I believed my path would be revealed to me.

I applied to seminary school that summer and was accepted. Now I had a decision to make. I was all set to start my doctoral studies the coming winter.

Could I do both? I played with the thought for a while, thinking that if I kept busy enough, it would help me heal or keep my mind off of my heart for enough time to pass. Time heals all wounds, right?

But something had to give. I struggled for weeks with my choice. My decision to pursue my doctorate was not a decision I had taken lightly. I had thoroughly researched universities that offered both the program I wanted and had the right mix of in-class and online courses that I believed would work with my schedule. Earning my doctorate degree was a lifetime goal, and I had worked hard, very hard, to fulfill the requirements and earn acceptance into a prestigious university.

Finally, at a loss as to what to do, I pulled out my journal. Turning to a new page, a page without prior constraints or expectations imbued in it, I titled it "Doctorate," drew a line down the middle, and labeled "Pros" on the left and "Cons" on the right. I created a second page and labeled it "Seminary." I would do this the old-fashioned way. I would write the pros and the cons to each program and compare.

I filled the "Pros" column for my doctoral studies with things like "more money, more prestige, a promotion, fulfilling a lifelong goal." My "Pros" column for seminary studies was filled with things like "feels right," "I keep smiling," and "I really want to do this!"

I didn't even make it to the "Cons" side of the list. I realized the doctoral program made me feel adult and practical, and the seminary program made my heart leap with joy and hope. At that point in my life, after what I had already been through, I chose joy and hope. I declined my admission into the doctoral program that afternoon.

Anticipation filled the rest of my summer. I knew that I had made the right choice when, for no apparent reason, I would catch myself smiling. That simple act gave me hope.

As the first leaves on the trees had begun to change colors in preparation for the next season of their lives, I was also preparing. Seminary had begun, and it was fascinating—touching and challenging every aspect of my person, intellectually, emotionally, and spiritually.

Every month, through study, discussion, writing, practice, and attending services at places of worship, I was experientially introduced to a different world religion or practice. The first month, while studying Buddhism, I attended a meditation at a local Tibetan Buddhist center.

Sitting cross-legged on a floor mat, in a dim candlelit room, I breathed in the stillness, the quiet. Before me, with his head slightly lowered in a bow, was the gentlest of souls. A Buddhist monk, wearing a traditional saffron robe, a bright orange color with a red sash draped loosely across his chest, sat cross-legged in front of me. His voice no louder than a whisper, he spoke of peace, the kind of peace that comes from going inward and releasing our attachment to the physical experience. He explained that experience is our teacher, and when we can honor our experience and release our attachment to it, we can find peace; we can find God.

"The first step is to realize that our experiences are opportunities to learn," he offered to our eager hearts. "We need to remove the judgment of the experience, for there is no good or bad. There just is."

"But what about tragedies, or situations that are so obviously unjust?" a man questioned. "How is that an opportunity to learn?"

The monk quietly replied, "Do not judge the person or the situation. You may not understand the why, but it is not for you to judge. Be of service, but release your attachment to the outcome. All experiences are an opportunity for your soul to learn."

I like that. No judgment. No good or bad. Just flow like the rhythm of a dance.

I considered my experiences in the past couple of years surrounding the breakdown of my marriage. *If our experiences are our teachers, then I sure am learning a lot.* But my soul responded to the ring of truth in his words, a truth that I could not deny. The lens on my Self-perception started to shift that evening. *If my experiences are my teachers, then maybe the rejection I felt as their result wasn't a personal commentary of my worth?* In his words I found a glimmer of hope, hope that deep down, my experiences did not define me—and that I did have value.

Studying Hinduism the next month also fascinated me. The Hindu belief in past lives was something that my Roman Catholic upbringing had not embraced. But it was a belief that always lingered at the far corners of my logical and spiritual brain. It didn't make sense to me that in a universe billions of years old, our lives were mere decades in the physical form. I was ready and excited to explore this further.

I had been curious about past-life regressions for

a while. I had read books on past-life regression, and I knew people who had done them. I learned that understanding what had happened in a past life could help you heal from trauma, negative feelings, and phobias in this life.

However, even though I believed in them and felt ready to experience a past-life regression, it had to be with someone I felt comfortable with, someone I trusted. As with everything else, I believed my angels were with me, guiding me—this time to Maria.

Maria Castillo, a licensed clinical social worker and past-life regression therapist, also attended the interfaith church that I did. She is a kind and welcoming woman with a warm and engaging smile, and we quickly became friends.

One day after service, during announcements, Maria shared that she would be holding a past-life regression at our church. It would be held in a group setting the next Friday night.

Oh my goodness! My mind raced. *This is what I have been waiting for.*

My study of Hinduism had reignited my interest and prepared me for this next logical step. I knew I was ready for it, and Maria's kind manner gave me the confidence to go forward. My only question was about projection, that my mind would somehow fabricate my experience. I wanted to be sure my regression would be authentic. I cornered Maria right after service with my concern.

"Maria! I am so excited to hear that you are going to hold a past-life regression! I would love to do it!" My words eagerly spilled from my lips. "But I have a question I hope you can answer."

"I am so glad you would like to participate, Patty." Maria smiled. "What is your question?"

"It's about projection. I have not done a past-life regression yet because I was afraid that I would project my own thoughts into it. How will I know what I can believe?"

"Your Higher Self will show you what you need to see," Maria explained. "If it is something that is familiar to you in some way, it is because your Higher Self was already making it known to you, through your thoughts, your dreams, or what we call 'coincidences.'

"You do not project your own thoughts into the regression. However, you are remembering through the lens of your current mind. So when you are speaking out loud about the memories during your regression, your conscious mind is filtering what the subconscious, or the Higher Mind, is remembering."

Her explanation resonated with me and removed my last concern. I signed up on the spot.

The next week seemed to drag on interminably, but finally, Friday night arrived, and I and eleven other spiritual seekers showed up for the regression with pillows and blankets in hand. The sanctuary space was quiet—peaceful, really—a direct contradiction to the anticipation that filled my being. A few soft lights and many candles radiated a soothing energy and beckoned me to breathe, to relax, and slow down my beating heart. My body reflexively listened, and as a deep breath filled my lungs, I breathed in the fragrance of lavender and lemon that filled the air. Needing a moment to take it all in, I took a seat in the back of the room. As I quietly observed the others getting settled, the peaceful feeling enveloped me fully and removed the last vestiges of my concern.

The group of people, my companions for the evening, silently busied themselves: arranging their spaces, taking out their journals, finding the elusive pen to write with, and mentally preparing for the experience to come. Their looks were varied, most nondescript like me—dressed in jeans and T-shirts, sweatpants and sweatshirts, comfortable clothes that would not encumber them or their experience.

However, in the far right corner of the room, a woman stood out to me. Not so much because of anything she did—or the way that she looked, although her long, kinky platinum-blond hair was attractive—but because of her pillow. The woman in the far right corner of the room had the most beautiful purple pillow. Silk, it looked like. A deep-purple silk pillow with iridescent blue beads adorning one side. I was distracted by her and her pillow until Maria's voice roused me out of my reverie.

"Welcome, everyone! Please leave your things where they are and come join me in the circle." Maria smiled and motioned to a group of chairs arranged in a circle at the end of the room. "It is time to begin. Tonight, I will lead you through three regressions. The first regression will be to your time in the womb, and then I will lead you into two past lives.

"But before we begin, to help us center and quiet our minds, we will practice some breathing and centering exercises. Please, take a deep breath, close your eyes, and start counting silently backward from one hundred, but count in increments of three, like so: one hundred, ninety-seven, ninety-four, ninety-one . . . ."

I closed my eyes, took a breath, and started to count. *One hundred, ninety-seven, ninety-four, ninety-one, eighty-eight, eighty-five, eighty-two, seventy-nine* . . . . All thoughts left my head, and my mind was focused solely on what the next number was going to be.

"Now let's try another one," Maria continued. "Breathe and close your eyes. Picture your thoughts moving by your eyes as if carried by the wind. They are traveling past your eyes too fast for you to focus on them. They just keep moving."

This exercise worked better than the first one. I couldn't attach myself to my thoughts because they kept moving. My mind was easily emptied of distractions.

The practice went on for a few more moments, and then Maria asked us to spread out around the room.

"Get your pillow and blanket and find a place that you feel comfortable," Maria instructed.

I found my private space in the back against a far wall. Since I wasn't sure what to expect, I wanted to be as private as possible. I settled in, pillow under my head and blanket wrapped around me, creating a cocoon. Finally, I said a silent prayer, asking my angels to support me and allow me to have the full experience.

"You will be conscious the entire time, and if anything happens that troubles you, you can just open your eyes," Maria reminded us. "Your conscious and subconscious mind will both be active. You can release any concerns and just allow the experience. You are safe and supported."

The lights dimmed further; we closed our eyes, and soft music played in the background. Maria, with a serene tone and a soothing cadence to her voice, began a meditation, like the ones we practiced to calm our breathing and clear our minds from distracting thoughts. My heartbeat slowed down to a steady, rhythmic beat, slower and slower until my mind quieted and I was centered inward.

We were ready to begin.

CHAPTER 6

I am standing on the top of a magnificent staircase, which reaches high into the breathtaking blue sky that surrounds it. The staircase is white marble, and the steps curve downward in a long graceful sweep, connecting the sky to the earth. With one hand resting lightly on the banister, I slowly descend. As I reach the last step, a lush garden springs up around me. There are colorful flowers of all varieties: some large and some tall, straining their ginger and golden faces to feel the warmth of the sun, and others content to sprawl along the garden floor, creating a patchwork of scarlet and violet. Butterflies flit by, and birds sing a chorus of melodies in the trees. As I breathe in the scents of the life all around me, a smile graces my lips. Feeling safe and secure, I walk into my garden, my fingertips caressing the tips of the flowers as I pass. As trees start to dot the edges of my vision, a bubbling stream becomes visible at my feet. I walk along the soft earth beside the stream and find a bench to rest on. Breathing deeply, I look out over the horizon. The sun is starting to set, blazing a deep fire of color across the sky. I rest for a moment but know that time is getting short. Not too far ahead, at the entrance to the forest, I see a gate. It is painted white and arched at the top. The most beautiful white light is shining through the diamond-shaped openings of the lattice work. Excited, I hurry forward, knowing that when I step through the gate, I will be in my mother's womb.

As I step through the gate and into the light, I am in an enclosed space. It is dark but not black or gray, more of a dark reddish brown. Maria asks us to look around and observe. I immediately see a long, almost comet shaped, pink-and-purple light. The light is moving quickly, flitting around, and is a distinct contrast to the dark reddish-brown walls. I can see through the eyes of the light, and with that comes the realization that I am the light.

What is going on? What am I doing wrong? I thought I was supposed to be in the womb?

Maria speaks again. "What do you feel? Do you hear anything? See anything more?"

Do I see anything? You mean besides the pink-and-purple light? *My mind races, sure I am doing something wrong.*

Wait! I do see something! It's a baby! *A sense of relief fills me as I realize that I am in my mother's womb.*

I understand that the baby is me. The baby in the womb is me. I, as the light, am looking at myself in the womb.

However, I don't hear anything or feel anything. I merely observe the baby lying contentedly in the womb as I, the light, flit around it.

Maria started to speak. "It is time to come back. Start to say good-bye. I will count backwards from ten to one. When I reach one, you must go back through the gate and into your body.

"Ten . . . three, two, one . . . . You are now back in your body. Take a deep breath and slowly open your eyes."

That was incredible and disconcerting. I didn't

experience anything that I thought I would. In fact, I was sure I did the whole thing wrong.

Maria asked if anyone had questions or wanted to share. A few people explained how they could feel themselves in the womb. They felt cramped or tight. Some people said they heard and felt their mother's heartbeat. Others expressed that a deep feeling of peace came over them.

I didn't feel or hear any of that. I raised my hand.

"Maria, I think I did this wrong," I hesitantly started to explain, second-guessing myself. "I wasn't really in the womb. There was a baby in the womb, and I felt like it was me, but I was looking through the eyes of a pink-and-purple light. I was flitting around the baby in the womb."

Maria smiled at me. I wasn't sure if that was to make me feel less conspicuous or if she understood.

"Patty, you did everything right. You can't do this wrong. Whatever your experience is, it is what your Higher Self wants you to see," she reassured me.

"What you saw was yourself in your soul state," she continued. "You hadn't entered the womb yet. The baby in the womb was you. Souls have a choice to enter in and out of the womb in the early stages of pregnancy."

"That's really interesting. So my soul is a pink-and-purple color?" I asked, wanting to make sure I understood. "I have been told that my aura is a violet color, but what I saw in the regression looked different."

"Your soul colors and aura colors are different. You saw your soul colors."

I was relieved. I hadn't done the regression wrong. I was ready to do the next regression—this time, into a past life.

"OK. Everyone, please get comfortable again. We are going to start our first regression into a past life. The visualization in the beginning will be the same. I will lead you down the staircase, through the garden, and through the gate into the white light. This time when you go through the gate, instead of being in the womb, you will have regressed to a past life."

I settled in. I said a prayer, again thanking the angels for my last experience and asking that they continue to support me. I was amazed with the rich detail that came through in the visualization . . . with nothing more than Maria directing our path. We closed our eyes and were slowly led again through the garden and to the gate. I could see the white light shining, and I stepped through.

"Look down at your feet," Maria prompts. "What are you wearing?"

I look down. Very large male feet, wrapped in Roman sandals, greet my eyes. I blink and look again. With dismay, I see they are not only male feet but flat and with square toes. What?

Whose feet are these? I wonder, looking for my slender, feminine feet with toenails painted red.

This time, I have to be doing something wrong. I look down again, and again, I am greeted with the same very large flat male feet wearing Roman sandals.

Maria is speaking again. I have to pay attention.

"Where are you? Who do you see?" are some of her questions.

I am not able to focus, and I need a moment to process this information. An odd tingling creeps up my spine.

"What do you see?" Maria asks the group.

Her voice brings me back. I feel strange, but in this

lifetime, I am a man. Tearing my eyes away from my feet, I pick up my head and look around. It is Roman times—I believe during the height of the Roman Empire. I am wearing a short white toga that falls loosely to my knees and is tied at the waist with a belt of some kind. I look about thirty-years old and have short light-brown hair.

People are gathered in a public square. The day is hot, and grumbles from the crowd are getting louder and more frequent. I am standing in the front of a group of men wearing togas similar to mine, and facing us is a crowd of Roman soldiers dressed in full armor-plated breastplates and helmets. The tension between my group and the soldiers is palpable, but I stand straight and hold my head high. I am fearless, and a leader to the men standing behind me. Suddenly, before I can speak, there is a rustle in the crowd of soldiers. In a flash, an arm is raised, a body lunges forward, and a spear is thrust into my chest!

Maria is speaking again. "Leave this time and go forward in your life. Where are you now? What is happening?"

Again, I am confused. How can I go forward? Didn't I just get stabbed? Didn't I die? *I take a breath and try to clear my mind. I look around. I am not dead. Somehow, I survived, and I have recovered. I see myself resting; however, my confusion has taken up so much time that Maria is speaking again.*

"Go forward again to the end of this lifetime, to your death scene. What do you see?" Maria asks.

Refocused and calm, I go forward. I am an old man lying on a decorative concrete bench on a hillside overlooking a city. It is springtime: the ground is covered in lush green grass; the heat of the summer has not yet started to take its toll, and the cool air has a dewy feel, as if it had recently rained. My home, a lavish estate, is behind me, and my wife of many years is by my side. Her long gray, wavy hair reaches far down her back, worn loose today, with no adornments to restrain its beauty. Her hands are holding mine, and her eyes glisten with the tears she is holding back. She smiles at me, her gentle smile that I have loved for a lifetime, as she tries to mask the pain I know she is carrying in her heart. I am near death. I pull my gaze from hers and look over on the hillside where many adult people are gathered. They are my children and their spouses. Everyone is here for me, to say his or her good-byes. I am growing weary, but I am not afraid, as I am surrounded by love. I am content. My life has been a good one.

Maria speaks, "It is time to return to your body now. I will start counting backwards from ten to one. Say good-bye and start walking back through the gate. When I reach the count of one, you will be back in your body, and when you are ready, you can open your eyes."

I sighed and returned. People were talking. They were sharing their experiences, but I couldn't talk yet. I could still feel it. I could still feel the love. My Higher Self had shown me a happy lifetime when I lived with someone I loved very much and with whom I had a large, loving family. Two years post-divorce, and as I was just starting to feel better emotionally, I was overcome with gratitude and elated with the knowledge that I had experienced real, lasting love before. A stinging sensation pricked the corner of my eyes, and I sat in silence as my vision blurred, tears sliding down my cheeks.

As several more minutes of sharing went by, it became obvious that the regressions were very meaningful for many of the people there that night; however, some of the lifetimes remembered were more positive than others. My attention was drawn to the woman I noticed earlier, the woman with the purple pillow. Sitting off to the right, the pillow clutched in front of her, and the beautiful fabric wet from her tears, she rocked back and forth, her platinum-blond hair falling across her face. Maria also noticed her and asked her if she would like to share. Haltingly, the woman recalled for us a childhood filled with sexual abuse by her father, ending only with her taking his life. It was a sobering moment.

We took a quick break to regroup, and Maria soon explained that it was time to do the next regression. The process would be the same as before, and I felt certain that, having done two regressions—and coming to terms with the knowledge that I was previously a man—I would be able to relax and embrace whatever my Higher Self chose to show me.

I walk down my grand staircase, through the beautiful garden, past the stream, stepping through the gate and into the light. I look down at my feet and see tall, dressy dark-brown boots that lace up the front and come up to about mid-calf. A long deep-blue velvet coat with buttons up the front and a high stiff collar, the type worn in the United States in the early 1800s, keeps me warm. My hair is walnut brown, grown long, with pipe curls pulled up in the back so the curls cascade to just below my shoulders, reminiscent of hair adorning a porcelain doll, complete with a blue velvet hat capped with a feather. I am a young woman in my twenties, slender and attractive.

The clip-clopping sound of horses' hooves fills the air. As I look up, a carriage drawn by a large black horse moves slowly past. I am standing on a sidewalk in what I believe to be Boston, MA. A narrow cobblestoned street is before me, winding through the city's tightly-packed brick buildings. On the brown brick building across the street, an address marker catches my eye, and I know that is where I am going.

The baby in my arms starts to squirm, and my attention is diverted to my children. In addition to my baby, two young children, a boy and a girl, around four or five years of age, are with me. They are not twins but are close in age. My son looks very handsome in matching shorts and jacket. His fists are clenched, elbows bent, and a wide smile crosses his young face as he jumps with great zeal next to me, the way only little boys seem to do. My daughter looks very much like a little lady, dressed in a button-up coat similar to mine. Waiting patiently, she holds tightly onto my coat, her behavior much different than her active brother's. We are preparing to cross the street, and I call my son to my side and remind them to hold on to my coat as we cross. Smiling, I take a step, a young mother happy and busy with my young children.

Maria's voice interrupts my memory, and she asks us to move forward in this life. I take a deep breath and see myself lying on a twin-sized bed. The room is small and dark, lit only by an oil lamp on a side table and the last remnants of the sun's rays coming through the lone window. Hot and uncomfortable, my sweat is sticking my long, loose hair to my face. I scream out, and a woman comes to my side. It is time. I am in the final stages of labor and just about to give birth. My body writhes with pain as the midwife holds a cold cloth to my forehead, encouraging me with her words. The baby is coming, and with a final push, I witness the birth of my son. I am exhausted by the birth, but happy. Wrapping my son in a blanket, the midwife puts him in my arms. As I lay there welcoming my child, she asks me if I would like to see my husband.

"Of course!" I respond, eager to see him.

She hurries to get him. He has been waiting in the next room, and he quickly comes in. Taking my hand, he sits down by my side, and I look up at him, excited to share the birth with him. Looking into his eyes, I see into his soul, and I am not prepared for what I see. The eyes that are staring back into mine are those of my ex-husband Steve.

What? *my mind reacts.*

I don't want it to be Steve! I am upset, disappointed. How could it be Steve, the man that I am now divorced from, the man that did not love me enough to stay and try to work things out? Shaken, I try to come to terms with this. I look again into the eyes of my husband, who is so lovingly sitting by my side, hoping for a different response. Yes, it is most certainly Steve.

Maria's voice cuts through my thoughts, the haze of my disappointment. She asks us to go forward to our death in this life. I take a deep breath and try to move forward, no longer interested in learning anything more. I am completely shaken by the fact that my husband in my former life is my ex-husband in this life.

After a moment, with little enthusiasm to learn more, I move to my death scene. It is early morning, and I wake to the sweet smell of the honeysuckle vines by my window, still fragrant with the morning dew. My body aches, and it is difficult to get out of bed. I am content to lie here for a few more minutes, as I am feeling extremely tired, and it is so early that I have yet to hear the birds' morning songs. Rubbing the soreness from my hands, I am taken with my gnarled fingers and bulging blue veins; gone is the smooth unblemished skin of a younger woman. The tiredness begins to worsen and weigh on me like a heavy cloak. My eyelids are heavy, and I close my eyes, unaware that it is for the last time.

"It is time to return to your bodies," Maria soothingly speaks to us. "I will count down from ten to one. When I reach one, you need to return through the gate and back into your body."

Maria begins to count. I am not paying attention. I see something off in the distance, a golden light.

What is that light? I move toward it.

"Nine . . . eight . . . . Start to come back." *Maria is counting.*

I ignore her and move in the direction of the light. I am getting closer. I have to see what it is.

"Seven . . . six . . . ."

It looks like a person! I can't turn away. I am being inexplicably drawn forward. I continue toward the light.

Still in the distance, a person is standing tall and straight; his broad shoulders are thrust back, his head held high, and his legs parted but ramrod straight. A golden light is emanating from him and luminously radiating all around him. His strength and power are palpable. My excitement builds, and I continue forward. I can now see his wings, expansive and brilliant golden wings. He is an angel! He holds a long sword, pointed downward, in front of him. His stance and presence are powerful, but inviting, as I know there is no danger.

"Five . . . four . . . ."

I keep going forward; just like a moth drawn to a light, I am drawn to the figure. My breath catches as more golden beings begin to appear. On each side of him, one at a time, alternating left and right, golden beings appear. It is reminiscent of a panel of people standing on a dais. I feel that they are there to greet me, to welcome me. There is a familiarity to them, and I believe that I know them, but I am not close enough yet to see their faces.

"Three . . . two . . . . You're almost to the gate. At one, you will go through the gate and back into your body."

No! I don't want to go back. I want to go toward the golden beings. Every cell of my body is reaching toward them. I need to clearly see their faces! I want to talk to them! There is such a love and a warmth emanating from them that it makes me ache.

"One."

Pop! I go back, through the gate and into my body. Jarred by the suddenness, I was filled with disappointment and left with a deep longing. This was not where I wanted to be. I wanted to be with the golden beings.

Numbness and confusion enveloped me. People were talking, but I was not paying attention. Questions were running through my head. *Why didn't I have more time? Why couldn't I get closer?* and most importantly, *Who are they?*

I must ask Maria for an explanation. At the first opportunity I had, I raised my hand and relayed what had just happened. What Maria said next shocked me.

"Sometimes during a regression when we come to the end of a life, our soul wants to go forward to its soul state and not go back into the body. Your soul was being called forward. In between our physical lives, there is a spiritual realm we go back to. This is where we meet with our guides and reflect on our experiences in the physical state. It is there that we decide what the next step for our soul will be. This time is referred to as 'life between lives,' and the golden beings that you saw were either your soul family or your guides."

Yes, I instinctively knew she was right. I could *feel* the pull toward the golden light; it was familiar and welcoming. I knew I was supposed to go back to the gate and into my body, and I didn't care. I had to move toward the light. To me, this confirmed that we are so much more than our physical form.

I lay there, wrapped in my blanket; my muscles

released their tension, and as my head rested lightly on my pillow, a comforting warmth permeated my body, and an unexpected smile found its way onto my lips. I had much to contemplate, to process. I thought of my wife from Roman times as she gazed at me with a deep love in her eyes, and I knew that I had felt true and lasting love, which was a welcome balm to my raw and still-bleeding heart. My husband from Boston, although initially upsetting to me that it was my ex-husband Steve, confirmed for me the feeling I had all those years ago on that fateful Halloween night. The jolt that went through my body when his eyes first looked into mine was a deeper connection shining through, a recognition of my soul seeing an old friend. My golden angels, the beings from whom I felt such a profound pull . . . I knew I was connected to and guided by them. That was enough.

Contented to let the knowledge of our spiritual magnificence wash over me, I reveled in the fact that in one evening, I received absolute confirmation of my spiritual Truth. I was, and still am, a spiritual being. We are all spiritual beings, and we have incarnated many times to have physical experiences. But most importantly, on this night, I discovered that we are not alone. I had been shown that we not only travel through lives with other spiritual friends but are fully supported and guided by loving beings, such as my golden angels. My eyes filled with tears as this truth permeated my human shell and settled deep within my soul. The pain and the loneliness that threatened to suffocate me since the divorce was finally being released. I felt empowered and liberated.

CHAPTER 7

It is said, "Ask and you shall receive." Well, I asked for a greater spiritual connection, and I began receiving so much that it made my head spin. Not only did I continue with my seminary studies, I took workshops to learn more about angels, how to read angel cards, and how to conduct physical and spiritual healings on myself and others—with the angels' help. In addition, I also had many unusual encounters with animals, and as time has gone on, I have realized that the animals were acting as totems and were another way that I had been receiving messages and guidance from the Divine.

It was an extraordinary time full of learning and expanding my sense of Self. During this time, I had also been given direct Divine guidance on what and how to write for my first book. In February, right before my winter break, I had a dreamlike experience, and I was shown, chapter-by-chapter, what to write. The words started to flow out of me, and for the next four days, I wrote the majority of my book. During the next few months, I wrote and edited the full story.

I was so profoundly affected by my spiritual experiences and studies, in late spring, I resigned from my job as a teacher to follow my spiritual path. I was not sure what I should do or what my journey would look like, but I knew I must direct my efforts and intentions toward finding out. I honored my teaching contract and responsibilities to my students and finished out the school year. As a single mother with two children to put through college, my decision raised many eyebrows and concerns, but I knew in my heart that this was what I had to do. My first book, *God is in the Little Things: Messages from the Animals*, was just the beginning of the work that I would do.

As the school year came to a close, so did my first year of seminary studies. Reading sacred texts and participating in worship services from many different faith-based traditions had broadened my perspective and helped me to embrace the rich history we have as a human race and the wisdom available to us in teachings spanning many centuries and cultures. My heart was opened more deeply, broken wide open, in fact, by the unwavering love and understanding I found emanating from all of the faith-based traditions. Wherever I looked, whether Eastern or Western beliefs, ancient texts or modern-day revelations, belief in a God outside of yourself, a God within, no God at all, or a God found within Mother Earth and all of her beings, I found love.

I also found much love from my seminary brothers and sisters. We had grown close over the past year, coming together and supporting each other with open and loving hearts. Our year-end intensive, a four-day culminating retreat, was upon us, and my angels chose this special time to give me another message.

Held at a retreat center located in the peaceful landscape of eastern New York and surrounded on all sides by nature's serenity, our days were filled with much study, discussion, reflection, and ceremony. As something fun to do to relax and celebrate with each other, we were asked to share our talents in the form of a talent show. It would be held on the third night of the retreat. Many people signed up right away to sing, dance, recite poetry, or perform a comedy routine.

Ugh! I don't have any creative talents to share! What am I supposed to do?

"I'll just watch the others!" muttered a voice in the back of the room.

"What?" I whirled around. "This isn't required?"

"No. Encouraged, but not mandatory," my classmate said.

"OK, good!" I replied, feeling relieved. "I'll just watch it too!"

But over the next two days, the thought of the talent show kept nagging at me. If I really was learning and growing and trusting in the support of the Divine, then I needed to do things differently than I would have in the past. The talent show was an opportunity to fully participate in the life around me, knowing I was loved and supported.

On the day of the talent show, I decided to take the plunge. Mustering up my courage, I found Ellen, the show organizer, and asked if there was still room for me in the show.

"Sure, but I need to know definitely by three o'clock today. What are you planning on doing?"

"Well, I realized I do have a talent for writing, so I thought I would read an excerpt from my upcoming book. But I don't have anything printed," I halfheartedly shared.

"No problem! There are computers and printers by the front desk. Just ask them for the password," Ellen replied.

"Great!" I said with more enthusiasm than I was feeling. The last excuse I had for not participating had just been resolved.

Since everyone had a three-minute time limit to share their talent, I scoured my first book to come up with a part that could accurately reflect the emotional aspect of my book and also share a message from one of the animals. I settled on an incredible encounter I had one morning with a toad, printed it out, and found Ellen to confirm I was going to do it.

"Perfect!" Ellen said, taking my introduction to read. "Let's see . . . I'll put you here, right after Samuel." Ellen inserted my name about halfway down the list of participants.

"Great!" I said, again with more enthusiasm than I was feeling. "See you at the show!"

The evening quickly came, and we all assembled in the large meeting room for the show. The participants were lined up against the right wall in the order they were to appear, and the audience filled in the seats. Anticipation hung in the air as Ellen, who was dressed in a striking green dress that matched her eyes, greeted everyone and introduced the first act.

I watched act after act. My seminary brothers and sisters were a very talented group, and they entertained us with songs, poetry, dance, and improv routines. With each performance and riotous laughs or cheers from the audience, my confidence faltered more.

What was I thinking, agreeing to read an excerpt for them? Not only is this a very talented group but they are spiritual seekers as well. What could I possibly share with them that they would find entertaining or meaningful?

By the time Samuel was getting ready to perform, I had worked myself into such a nervous self-doubting state that my heart was pounding visibly in my chest, and I thought I was going to be sick. Leaning against the wall for support, I asked my angels to help me get through it. Closing my eyes, I half listened as Ellen introduced Samuel.

"This little light of mine, I'm gonna let it shine! This little light of mine, I'm gonna let it shine. This little light of mine . . ." Samuel sang, his deep voice resonating through the room.

My eyes snapped open! I couldn't believe it. Samuel was singing the same song my angel Clarice sang to me in my first angel reading! And he was singing it directly before I was to read!

"Let it shine, let it shine, let it shine!" The audience joined in for a resounding finish.

My angels were supporting me and telling me that I did have value, and my work was meaningful, and that it was okay to step up in front of my seminary brothers and sisters and share a part of myself.

And I did. Still a little shaky at first, I started. By the time the reaffirming applause and loving words from the audience washed over me, my confidence was restored. As I sat down afterward to enjoy the rest of the show, I silently thanked my angels for being there for me once again.

CHAPTER 8

The summer solstice was upon us, and as the earth in the northern hemisphere prepared for the day when the light of the sun shines the longest, I too had been preparing for my light to continue to shine. Since the long, cold, dark days of winter when I took a beginning angel-healing course, I had been readying myself for this. The time had finally come for me to take the second part of the training, the advanced angel-healing course.

In great anticipation, I drove to a neighboring town where the course was being held. Happily, I was reacquainted with my instructor, Marie Marchesseault. Greeting Marie warmly, I saw over her shoulder a shock of dark, reddish-brown hair in the next room. It was my friend and partner from the beginning course, a woman named Cathy. As I made my way in to greet her, I saw that she was speaking to an older woman who, I learned, had travelled very far for these teachings. The four of us were going to spend the next two days traveling The Crystal Path™, an advanced angel-healing workshop created by Walter Lübeck. The focus of the workshop was to build upon the knowledge learned in the beginning course and further develop our abilities to work with the energies of the angels.

We would also astral travel to the Lemurian seven heavens to receive specific spiritual healing. As the knowledge taught in the course was extensive and the structure of the seven heavens reflected Lemurian teachings from an ancient lost civilization, I cannot go into specific details. However, I have the ability to share my experience when I astral traveled to the seventh heaven and once again was met by my golden beings.

As we settled in with our cups of herbal tea to quench our thirst and calm our energy, Marie handed us our manuals. They were carefully put together with the information and mantras we would need to do our work, and we would refer to them frequently over the course of the next two days. To fully understand the material, the learning was experiential. We practiced everything with our own thoughts, feelings, and issues.

To travel to one of the seven heavens was to receive answers or healing related to an issue of some kind. Depending on the question or the issue presented, a different heaven is chosen to travel to.

At this time, I was having difficulties relating to one of my daughters. Even though much time had passed since the divorce, and I was emotionally feeling stronger and was much less susceptible to certain triggers, we often fell back into our old habit of arguing with each other. For no apparent reason, normal conversations would quickly turn into a disagreement. This had gone on for so long that I sought out help to heal, or clear, any negative energy that was surrounding us and impeding us from changing our behaviors.

To start the exercise, we were asked to write down a very specific request. I wrote "please help me to understand how my daughter and I can understand each other and release all judgments." I referred to my manual and found that based on the emotional and spiritual nature of my request, I was to travel to the seventh heaven for answers and healing.

Marie led us through a powerful group meditation to prepare us for travel to our respective heavens. Meditating, we visualized a five-pointed star in our mind's eye. The color of the star changed from red to orange to yellow to green to blue to violet to white—corresponding to the colors of our chakras. As the star turned to white, a doorway within the star opened; this was the portal into the Divine realm. We called on the heaven and its guides by name to meet us and to direct us. As we stepped through the doorway, we entered the specific heaven we had chosen and were met by our guide. The following was taken directly from my journal notes immediately after my experience:

Stepping through the portal, I find a landscape of green fields stretching far and wide, ultimately ending with the rising and falling of gently-sloping hills. Farther in the distance, I see a mountain range, its rocky brown peaks standing rigid and proud. Animals of all kinds dot the landscape, peacefully eating or lying down under the large yellow sun. As my feet touch the ground, butterflies and a large female deer appear directly in front of me. My eyes lock with the doe's soulful brown eyes, our gaze only broken by the butterflies flitting between us. The sky above is streaked with all colors, the most vibrant hues of pink, purple, yellow, and blue. To the left, I see a rushing river, expansive in size and its presence commanding. Its currents are strong as the dark-blue water rushes through the river's vast expanse. As I walk to the river, the fields and animals fall away as my gaze fixes upon people gathered by the river's edge. Walking closer, I see a golden light emanating from them, and I recognize them from my regression as my friends and guides in the spiritual realm. It reassures me and fills me with joy to see them. However, unlike the regression where I experienced an undeniable pull to go toward them, I feel strangely content to look upon them from afar, so I do not approach them.

Slowly, I walk along the mighty river until I reach its mouth, an immense pool met by a single stream that flows up and through mountains, directing my path. The mountains are still very far away, and only a golden glow rising from their peaks distinguishes the area that I am to travel to. Instinctively, I know that I am to go to the center of the mountains for my answers, and as it is a great distance, I need to wait for my guide to bring me.

The guides for the Lemurian seven heavens appear as dragons; some refer to them as real dragons, some refer to them as angels, and some refer to them simply as an archetypal energy. To me, it doesn't matter, as I accept all forms of energy as Divine. Very shortly, my guide, a majestic gold-and-black dragon, appears at my side. He is massive; his height is easily three times my own, and his folded wings extend down the full length of his body. His skin is covered in large, shiny scales of alternating colors of pure black and shiny gold. His presence is awe-inspiring, not frightening in the least, and I feel a startling familiarity with him.

Climbing onto his back, I wrap my arms as best as I can around his thick neck and hold on. Gently, he rises, his mighty wings unfolding to their full magnificence, and we soar through the sky, my guide and I, over the mountain peaks and toward the golden glow. The mountains are barren, the fertile green fields now gone. As far as my eyes can see, there are only large outcroppings and peaks of unexceptional brown rocks with arid dirt covering the ground.

My guide brings me directly to the center of the main ring of mountains and skillfully lands. I slide down his back and feel the solid ground beneath my feet. Standing in a large open area, circular in shape and with no vegetation in sight, I suddenly feel frightened. Not of a physical force, but frightened of what will be revealed to me. Visibly shaking, I turn back and hide my face in the dragon's body, the soft spot where his wing begins.

"I am afraid," I tell him.

He gently nudges me and tells me to look. I reluctantly pick up my head.

A baby is lying on the ground in the middle of the circle. Turning away and lowering my eyes, I question the dragon.

"What is happening?" I exclaim.

He tells me to look again. Hesitantly, I pick up my head and see a woman who had kneeled down on the ground, cradling the baby in her arms. She rocks back and forth, as if in mourning. I don't understand, but I feel sad and scared and hide my face against the dragon's cool and comforting scales.

"Patty, look again," he gently tells me.

"I don't understand! Please give me some understanding!" I plead with my guide.

I raise my eyes, and I am shown that the baby is dead and my daughter is the woman cradling her lovingly in her arms. There is a great sadness, heaviness, in the air, making it difficult to even breathe. Panicked, I run to try to comfort them, but my daughter does not acknowledge my presence, still rocking mournfully back and forth in her grief.

Confused and afraid, I run back to the dragon. Knowing in my heart that I am somehow to blame for the sadness, I once again hide my face. But I can't stay away; my love for my daughter is greater than my fear, and I have to go back, to try to help.

"Why doesn't she see me or hear my cries?" I plead, desperate for answers. But my pleas go unanswered, and I realize that it is up to me to act.

I run back once again, and as I come upon her and the baby, sorrow overwhelms me.

"Forgive me! Please forgive me!" Distraught, I beg them both. "I love you, and I am sorry!"

Falling to my knees and wrapping my arms around them, I cry with them, my body joining theirs, rocking back and forth in rhythm to their motion.

"I love you, and I'm sorry," I say, repeating it between sobs.

The dragon comes and protectively wraps his wings around us. Tears stream down my cheeks as my anguish grows stronger, heartbroken by the sadness enveloping us and guilty because I realize I am somehow involved. There is still no recognition from my daughter, and I know it is not enough; we need something greater than ourselves to heal our hearts.

As my thoughts form, the golden beings from the river appear. Slowly, they come forward from the outskirts of the clearing. Surrounding us, they wrap us all in their love. I beg for forgiveness again. The beings' glow intensifies, and their golden light emanates from them, encircling and enveloping us. We are all filled with the golden light, the pain lessening with each instant that passes. We stay in the light, all of us, locked together in love and forgiveness."

All too soon, it was over, and I was back in my body. I gulped for air, trying to stop my steady stream of tears as I furiously wrote in my journal, determined to remember every instant. I still don't fully understand all that I was shown, and how I was involved, but the love that I felt from the golden beings was immense. Gratitude filled me, and my heart told me that together, my daughter and I had received a deep healing.

CHAPTER 9

The long-held perceptions I had of my Self and my human experiences were changing. My knee-jerk reactions to situations and feelings no longer came solely from my ego or my human perspective but, oftentimes, from my spiritual Self. I was beginning to look at myself and others through the lens of my Spirit, and trust that I was fully supported by loving spiritual beings. The realization that things were not happening to me, but for me, was profound. I could begin to look back on the pain I had gone through, and the uncertainty I still felt, and see the opportunity for learning my soul had asked for.

As the long hot summer wound down, my first book, *God is in the Little Things: Messages from the Animals,* had just been published. I was excited for this new phase in my life, and I was eager to share the healing messages and learning I had experienced.

One bright sunny Sunday morning, I was leaving the gym on my way to meet Lynette for lunch. As I drove to the interfaith center to meet her, I was distracted by a sudden tightness and pain in my neck. Making a mental note to schedule a massage, I was surprised by my very next thought. *I need to call Maria because it is time for me to do another past-life regression.* Since that seemed to come to me out of thin air, and as they seemed to be two completely unrelated thoughts, I chalked it up to my multitasking brain being on overload. I would soon discover that it was really Divine intervention.

Arriving at the center, I was greeted by Lynette. She was talking to a tall, thin gentleman whose gray hair was pulled back into a short ponytail.

"Hi, Patty!" Her bright brown eyes glanced over the gentleman's shoulder, and she welcomed me with a smile. "Have you met Bruce Smith, our new massage therapist?"

I vaguely remembered someone telling me about a new therapist at the center. They said he did a type of energetic massage—a traditional massage combined with energy work to bring balance and wellness to the client.

"No, we haven't met. It's nice to meet you. I'm Patty," I said as he turned around to face me, and I extended my hand out to shake his. As his hand clasped mine, I looked into his clear-blue eyes and noticed the laugh wrinkles embedded in the corners. A sweet smile appeared on his lips.

"This is so funny," I said, "because as I was driving here, I thought that I needed to schedule a massage. My neck is very tight. You wouldn't happen to have any availability, would you?" I grinned.

"Actually, I just had a cancellation today. Does two o'clock work for you?" Bruce asked with a smile.

As Divine timing would have it, it was just before noon, and Lynette and I were going to lunch. My kids were away for the weekend, and I had the rest of the day to myself.

"Two o'clock is perfect!" I exclaimed. "Thank you! I am so grateful you can fit me in. How weird is it that you just had a cancellation?"

Bruce smiled again and, with a twinkle in his clear-blue eyes, said, "Not weird at all. You know there are no coincidences."

At his words, a quiver went down my spine. I agreed.

Lynette and I left, and we had a wonderful time enjoying a delicious lunch at a nearby pizza place. Happy for the time spent with Lynette, I was also anxious to get back, to see Bruce and have my massage. When two o'clock came, I raced back to the center. The pain in my neck had worsened, but mostly, my anticipation for what was to come had increased.

Bruce met me in the outer office and explained more to me about an energetic massage.

"I will massage your body, Patty, but not specifically only your muscles. I will also work on the energy points throughout your body to clear stuck energy, which really causes much of our physical discomfort. I will also energetically clear, charge, and cap your chakras."

I knew that our chakras are our energy centers, and they reside in our subtle, or spiritual, bodies, which are mirrored by our physical body. According to my studies, there are seven main chakras, and they are capable of giving and receiving energy. I had been taught that to be in optimum health—physically, mentally, emotionally, and spiritually—the chakras have to be cleared of any limiting beliefs or blocks.

Great! This was even more than I was hoping for. As I had more and more spiritual experiences, I firmly believed that much, if not all, of the pain and sickness in the physical body is a result of an imbalance in our emotional or spiritual body. I was eager to start.

The lights were dimmed, and soft instrumental music was playing in the background. Lying face down on the massage table, Bruce worked his magic on my neck, back, and legs. I could tell right away that this massage was different than others I have had because Bruce didn't just rub certain muscles, but also held or pushed on what seemed to be pairs of points along my body. I decided not to question but to just relax into my breath and the stillness of the room.

"Please turn over," Bruce gently requested, rousing me from the tranquility of my mind. "I will now begin the clearing of your chakras."

Opening my eyes, I slowly, almost grudgingly, turned over as my mind returned to the present moment. I breathed deeply, anticipating the chakra clearing. I have had my chakras cleared before and always welcomed the opportunity. I have likened it to a tune-up of my energetic body. Just as our muscles can get sore, or our spines out of alignment, and require a massage or chiropractic adjustment, so do our chakras require attention to function fully.

Knowing how important the clearing and balancing of our chakras are, I took another deep breath, closed my eyes, and was ready to begin. I lay quietly, and to help facilitate the clearing, I visualized my body being surrounded by the green, healing light of Archangel Raphael, the archangel that helps with physical, emotional, psychological, and spiritual healing. Raphael's light is green, and inviting him to be with you and surround you with his light is a healing process, according to my studies.

Starting at the top of my head, my crown chakra, I could feel Bruce whispering and gently moving his hands over my chakra points. Nothing stood out to me as extraordinary until Bruce came to my heart chakra, located in the center of the chest. Here, his movements became stronger, and I felt like he was trying to pull something out of me. He seemed to stay at my heart chakra for a long time. I assumed that I had to clear out more of the hurt that I had experienced from my divorce, and I breathed deeper, asking Archangel Raphael to assist Bruce in the clearing.

After what seemed to be a very long time, Bruce finished with my heart chakra and continued to my solar plexus. The rest of the chakra clearing went on uneventfully. All too soon, my massage ended, and I heard the dreaded words: "You can get dressed now."

Reluctantly, I stretched and breathed and slowly rolled off the massage table, not yet ready to leave the stillness that I had retreated to. Gently shaking my head to bring my focus back to the present, I got dressed. Joining Bruce in the waiting room, he handed me a cup of water to drink, looked deep into my eyes, and explained what was happening at my heart chakra.

"You have a very deep anger inside of your heart," Bruce began. "I tried to clear it, but I couldn't. I believe it is very old and not from this lifetime. It is something you must clear for yourself."

Funny enough, his words did not surprise me; a tingling of recognition went down my spine. My mind immediately recalled a walk I took about a year prior with my dog Bear, my faithful and sweet black curly-haired Cockapoo.

One cloudless winter day, under the bluest of skies, Bear and I were enjoying one of our regular walks through our neighborhood. Bear excitedly pranced with his head held high, as if he were a prince surveying his kingdom, and his short tail wagged, showing his happiness and approval, and I talked to him and laughed as I watched him.

All of the sudden, I was stopped midsentence, as I had a distinct vision of something very black inside of me. It was dark and round, about six inches in diameter, and located in the area of my abdomen. It rattled me, as I didn't know what it was, but I knew that it was something I did not want. Immediately, I asked my angels for an explanation and knew intuitively that it was something within me that was unresolved. I tried to visualize healing white light surrounding it and removing it from my body, but I was unable to; the blackness remained.

I was not frightened of it, as I knew it was a message for me, and after a few moments, the vision of the blackness went away. The issue wasn't yet cleared, and I got a strong sense that I had more to understand before I could clear it. When it was time, I would know.

I knew without a doubt that the anger Bruce spoke of was the blackness that I saw. I also understood why I considered calling Maria and doing another past-life regression at the same time that I thought of having a massage.

I explained everything to Bruce. He also wasn't surprised, having had much experience with Divine intervention himself. He said he would like to see me in two weeks. Doing the past-life regression before our next appointment would be helpful, but it was not necessary. I made an appointment to come back to see him in two weeks.

Leaving the massage office, I was filled with an overwhelming sense of gratitude. Bruce was right: there are no coincidences, and I could once again feel the support and guidance of my angels. I was excited to see Maria, but I also knew in my heart that I didn't need to call her right away. I would see her when I was supposed to. I was learning to release some of the control I tried to hold over my life and simply allow the Divine to work with me. Also, my first book had just been published, and I was busy promoting it. Having had no experience in the fields of publishing and promotion, I spent most of my time trying to figure it out, and I knew that was what I needed to focus my attention on.

My first book signing was being held at the local farmers market that coming Friday. I was excited and also apprehensive. It was one thing to write my personal story, warts and all, from the privacy of my home and sell it anonymously over the Internet. But it was something entirely different to show up in person and talk to my neighbors and community members about it. But I knew in my heart that I had to do it. I had to stand in my Truth as a spiritual being and proudly share my story and my book. The experiences I had—and was still having—happened for a reason, and the messages of Spirit and healing were mine to share.

The last Friday in that August was gorgeous, a rare summer day when the humidity levels were low and you could comfortably sit outside and enjoy nature. I took the weather as a good sign, took a deep breath, and filled my car with books. Saying a quick prayer, I set off for our local farmers market, which was situated on a quintessential New England green: a large space of land in front of the town hall and surrounded on two sides by churches built in the 1700s. A white gazebo was the centerpiece of the green, which has been a gathering place for town residents for hundreds of years.

Busily setting up and chatting with the other vendors, I was pleasantly surprised when I heard a familiar voice.

"Hi, Patty! I had a few minutes between clients, and I ran over to see you and get your book!" Maria exclaimed. "I was hoping you would be here early!"

"Maria! I can't believe you are here! I am so happy to see you!" I hugged her as I spoke. "I was planning on calling you," I continued. "I need to see you. It is time for me to do another past-life regression, and this time, I think I need to do a private session."

"Sure, whatever you need. Let me check my calendar, and I'll call you next week."

"Perfect. Thank you," I replied, hoping she could fit me in before my next appointment with Bruce but knowing in my heart that it would happen when it was supposed to.

Maria called early the next week. Not surprisingly, she told me that she just had two people cancel for the coming Friday morning and had a two-hour block free, the time needed to do a private regression.

"I'll take it!" I said, silently thanking my angels for their help once again.

CHAPTER 10

Grayness. I am ensconced in a cloudy, misty, grayness. Swirling dullness—just dense enough to obscure my vision. I feel like I am stuck, emotionally unable to move forward. As my stress amplifies, the muscles in my body begin to contract. Maria asks me to look down, to look at my feet, to help determine who and where I am. I follow her instruction, but there is nothing to see except more seemingly endless and indistinguishable grayness.

"There is only grayness. I can't see anything!" My words sputtered out through my tightened lips and constricted throat.

"Do you hear anything?" Maria calmly asks, her demeanor a stark contrast to my own.

Her calmness soothes me, and I strain to listen. Yes! I hear music; classical music is being played, but it is faint and far away. As I move through the mist and toward the music, I hear people talking off in the distance. Their voices are muffled, but laughter rings out, and it sounds like a party. Anxious, I move closer . . . .

My private past-life regression with Maria had begun. I had shared with Maria my desire to be shown the past life where I felt such a deep anger. Maria explained that we can ask our Higher Selves to show us specific lives, but there is no guarantee. Our Higher Selves will show us what it feels we need to see.

I understood. I have had enough experiences on my journey to trust fully in the Divine. Whatever I would see would be for my highest and greatest good. I silently asked my angels to stay with me and support me fully in my experience.

Anxious, I move closer. The mist begins to clear, and I am outside in the country standing on a large expanse of lawn. The perfectly-manicured green lawn is met by an endless sapphire-blue sky above. A large white house, more like a rambling country estate, is to the left, and a beautiful white gazebo is straight ahead, where a quartet of musicians plays the melodic tunes that drew me here.

People standing in small groups fill the lawn, drinks in hand, smiling and talking. Dressed in elegant attire—the women fashionable in long dresses and fancy hats that shade their delicate skin, and the men in suits, proper and distinguished, as reserved in their dress as they are in their demeanor. Curious, I look down at myself and notice shiny black shoes and a pinstriped suit that frames my slim build. A man in my mid-thirties, my hair and mustache are still thick and jet-black in color. It is the early twentieth century, and the party is at a colleague's country estate. I work in finance, and I live in New York City, and like the rest of the people at the party, I am doing well financially.

In spite of the gaiety, I am disconcerted as a foreboding fills my body. I am a guest at the party, but I do not feel connected with the people, and an uncomfortable prickling ac-

centuates the separateness. Nearby is a group of four women that look about my age. Whispering animatedly, their heads close together, they glance up at me as I approach, only to greet me with contemptuous sneers and angry glares. Stopped in my tracks by their hateful behavior, I am at a loss as to the reason why.

Out of the corner of my eye, a figure catches my attention. It is a woman standing with two young boys; holding their hands, she casts her gaze downward. Mousy-brown hair frames her face, and her simple white blouse and long tan skirt is in stark contrast to the rainbow of colorful and fashionable dresses worn by the other women. With her slight build and shoulders turned inward, she seems physically and emotionally weak and small. I am shocked by the knowledge that she is my wife and the young boys are my sons.

I know that I don't respect her, and I have a vision of her cowering, her slight build and presence reduced even more. I realize that I have harmed her, and I am troubled by the fact I am physically and emotionally abusive to my wife. With this knowledge, a sharp pain shoots through my stomach as if I have been punched in the gut.

My wife lives in fear of me, and the more fearful she is, the angrier I become. I resent her weakness, and as my agitation increases, I frustratingly repeat over and over, "She is weak; she is so weak."

Maria asks me to move forward in this life. It is a few years later. I feel out of sorts, agitated still. The pain in my stomach remains. My wife has died. I'm not sure how she died, but I believe it was because she was so physically and emotionally weak. I know she didn't have a happy life with me. I am angry at her. I am angry that she died. I don't know why I chose her as my wife and why, or if, I loved her. She became so weak, and the weaker she became, the more I resented her. My sons are twelve and thirteen, and I don't know who is supposed to take care of them now. I feel that I have been cheated, and I am very angry and resentful.

I move forward to my death. Lying on my bed, I am left with only the bone-rattling cough of pneumonia beating up my frail body. In the last moments of my life, there is only me. My sons and a nurse are physically in the room, but they are not with me. Their sense of duty makes them stay, but we are all eager to leave. The nurse, eager to leave behind an irritating and difficult patient; my sons, eager to leave behind an unlovable, resentful man they had the misfortune to call their father; and I, eager to leave this miserable place filled with bitter disappointments. With a final, bone-shattering cough, my body finally dies.

I lie there and hold my stomach, as the pain has increased. I believe it is a physical manifestation of the shame that I feel. Maria asks me if I would like to do another regression or visit my guides, my spiritual family that supports and guides me.

"I need to see my guides," I say over and over. "I need to somehow resolve these feelings."

"I agree. Go to them now," Maria encourages me.

Innately, I know where to go and how to get there. I start to ascend up into the sky. I am a light again, a thin, long comet-shaped pink-and-purple light. My ascension should be easy and quick, but it is not. I am carrying an immense burden, and I am weighed down by my shame and guilt. I strain to rise up, my physical body reflexively lifting slightly off the couch in support. The air around me is thick, and I feel attached to the earth. Tears engulf me as I battle against invisible cords. My shame is overwhelming to me, and I try to breathe through my tears, knowing that I need to reach my guides. Struggling, I push on, and little by little, with great difficulty, I ascend. It is an enormous effort, the immensity of my feelings a burden on my soul, but finally, I gratefully leave the sky and cross into the spiritual realm.

I am lighter here; the cloak of heaviness lifted somewhat when I crossed into this realm, but the shame and guilt remain. For a moment, I stand alone, darkness all around me, and I am not sure what to do. But very quickly, I see a golden light approaching. Its radiance becomes more brilliant with each passing moment, and soon, the entire area is illuminated. Golden beings—my guides that have been with me before—step forward. My breath catches, and I hesitate, unsure of what they think. But my hesitation lasts only for an instant as they surround me. Hugging me, they once again envelop me in their light and their love.

Tears stream down my cheeks as I feel their loving energy. I am in great conflict, as their loving actions accentuate the shame I feel. How do I deserve this love, considering my actions in my previous life were cruel and caused great harm? I send out a silent plea to them. My guides reassure me that I am worthy and that all is forgiven, as our human actions do not validate or invalidate the worth of our Spirit. "You are not broken and you do not need to be fixed," they lovingly express. "You are whole and you are perfect." Complete acceptance and love seep into my soul.

With this understanding, my light starts to grow bigger; my long, thin comet-shaped light expands larger and taller. My shape takes a human form, and as I stand in my fullness, I am so tall that I look like a giant. Towering over the golden beings, they now back away and encircle me from a distance. They are smiling. They are pleased. I realize that they are truly my friends, more than my guides.

Lovingly, they explain that because of my guilt and shame, I had dimmed my light. Accepting their love, and understanding my true worth, my light is getting brighter again. In my completeness, I stand tall—an enormous pink-and-purple being with beautiful wings of my own. There is a golden light, a candle of sorts that is flashing up within me, making me glow from the inside. I am humbled and so grateful to be a witness to my Self.

Suddenly, a figure comes through the circle toward me. It is Jesus. He tells me that he is happy that I remember and understand my true Self. He says that he is glad that I am finally back. His words make me realize that I, as my true Self, have been gone a long time. Jesus hugs me and leaves.

Other lights are around me now—smaller white lights. They appear to be younger souls, and they are dancing. Being as small as they are, they only come up to the bottom of my wings. Running and dancing joyfully in circles around me, I know that I am a teacher to them, a guide for them. They are happy and excited that I am back, and it is cause for a celebration.

As I stand there, with the younger souls celebrating around me and my golden beings encircling us in a wider circle, the enormity of what I have learned begins to sink in. My light was diminished for so long because of the shame and the guilt I felt by my actions in my previous life. I diminished my own light. I was not unlovable, and I was not being punished. For with Spirit, there is no punishment; there is only love. Once I saw my true Self and I accepted the love given freely from my guides, I could start to love and forgive myself. I understood why I felt so unlovable in this lifetime and where my anger was coming from. I could now begin to heal.

I want to stay longer, but Maria tells me it is time to leave. My guides tell me that I must go because I have much work to do.

"But before you go, tell me what your name is. What do they call you?" Maria asks.

"Ariel," I say without hesitation.

CHAPTER 11

"It is not often that a soul sees a lifetime in which they behaved in a hostile way," Maria shared with me. "It is hard for us to accept that we could behave in such a way, but I can assure you that every soul has lifetimes in which they act negatively.

"It is part of our soul's journey to experience the physical realm and feel the emotions, both the positive and the negative, associated with it."

I thanked her for her words and left, still feeling very unsettled. I had a lot to process. There was no escaping that many things in the regression rang true for me. Although I have never been physically abusive to anyone in this lifetime, I have struggled with impatience and anger. One of my biggest pet peeves: someone who didn't seem to be working hard enough or trying to help improve their situation. I would get impatient if I felt someone was weak in any way. Until very recently, I am embarrassed to say that I lived my life with little compassion for people who have struggled with something. I couldn't, or wouldn't, understand why they didn't help themselves, and many times, I expressed my frustration.

They should just pick themselves up by their bootstraps and keep going or *they should stop feeling sorry for themselves* were frequent criticisms of mine.

So I could see vestiges of my anger in this lifetime. I could also see that the feelings of shame and guilt that I had felt from this prior life were my feelings of "not good enough" and lack of self-love in this life. Intellectually, I got it. Dealing with it, emotionally, was a little more difficult.

Randomly, throughout the weekend, my stomach would hurt and tears would well up in my eyes as I thought of my wife from my previous lifetime and the pain that I had caused her. My entire perception of myself as a "good" person, one that would never consciously harm anyone, had been turned upside down. I replayed the healing messages, which I had received from my guides, over and over in my mind and told myself that I was forgiven, that everything was all right. But I still felt different in my own body, like I had on clothes that didn't fit.

With a jolt, I also realized that the recurring pain in my stomach was in the same place that I had seen the blackness the previous year. I was eager to see Bruce, as I hoped he could help energetically clear away some of my disturbing thoughts and feelings, thereby clearing the blackness and my pain for good.

Arriving at my appointment, Bruce asked how I had been. I told him I was well. I didn't share that I had seen Maria or had the past-life regression. I wanted to have the massage and clearing without any prior discussion and see what came up for me, afraid that if I tried to control the situation by telling Bruce my thoughts, I would somehow circumvent Divine intention. In awe of what had already been shown to me, I believed that it was now time for me to simply allow the process to unfold.

Pushing my disquieting thoughts back into the far recesses of my psyche, I slowly undressed, savoring the moment and optimistic that my troubled mind would soon be eased. Sliding under the sheet, I rang the bell for Bruce to come in. With the light in the room dimmed and the music playing softly, I breathed deeply and relaxed into peaceful solitude.

The massage and clearing again felt wonderful, but this time, it seemed rather uneventful. Bruce still seemed to spend a lot of time at my heart chakra, but there was nothing unusual that I could put my finger on until we talked afterward.

"Well, how did I do?" I asked with a smile, trying to break the ice but still ask for information.

"Forgiveness... forgiveness... I kept hearing the word 'forgiveness'," Bruce replied.

CHAPTER 12

Timing is everything, they say. Divine timing is even more so. With Bruce's words still ringing loudly in my ears, the very next week I embarked on a spiritual journey of a lifetime. England, the magical land of Merlin and King Arthur, Stonehenge, and the Druids, had called me. Months prior, I had booked a journey with a spiritual teacher of mine, and I and a group of twenty-two spiritual seekers like me were now finally on our way.

Our home for the next week, a charming, centuries-old English inn, made the perfect backdrop for me to finally release some very old burdens. Late one afternoon, my friend Kamala and I had some time alone. Sitting on our beds in the room we shared, I found myself needing to talk. I was still processing—and most days, struggling with—what I had learned about myself in my last regression.

The love I had received from my guides was transformative in the way that I thought of my spiritual Self. However, the abusive and cruel actions performed by me in my human form were plaguing my heart. I hoped that speaking out loud all that had happened, and receiving positive reinforcement from another, would soothe my troubling thoughts and allow me to fully move forward.

So on a gray rainy September day, in our damp chilly room, in the old English inn, I shared everything: the regression, the healing and love I received from my guides, the blackness I saw in my abdomen and the unease and pain I had recently had, my two energetic massages, and the messages received. Kamala listened patiently, and when I finished, she asked me a very surprising question.

"Why didn't you do a healing?" she gently inquired.

"I did do a healing. I just told you I received an amazing one from my guides," I answered, not sure why she didn't hear me.

"No, why didn't you do a healing for your wife and for yourself?" she explained. "You need to ask forgiveness of your wife, and you need to forgive yourself."

Her words made my stomach ache once more. I knew what she said was true. I had wondered about the soul of my wife, but I tried to tell myself that her soul understood I was sorry. As for forgiving myself, well, I was still processing that. Many times since the regression, I found myself in tears, recalling my abusive behavior in my past life.

"How do I do a healing?" my soul seemed to ask for me.

"When I do past-life regressions with people, if something that needs healing comes up for them, we do the healing right then. By asking for forgiveness and giving forgiveness, we clear the imprints of the other lifetime on our current lifetime. This is a crucial step in healing alternate life issues. If you want, I can help you with it now," Kamala generously offered.

I was shocked. Even though Kamala and I were in seminary together and had become friends, there was a lot I didn't know about her. It turned out she was an amazing healer, and she was offering me a tremendous gift.

"Yes, I would love to do a healing, Kamala. Thank you," I gratefully accepted.

"Great! Lie down on your back on your bed and make sure you are comfortable," she instructed.

I did as I was told. I think I would l have laid down on a bed of rocks at that moment, desperately needing to resolve my pain.

"Do I have permission to check your chakras?" she asked.

"Of course you can. Do whatever you need to do," I replied.

Kamala proceeded to run her hand over the seven main chakras on my body. She did this for several minutes, scanning each one for any energy imbalance. When she finished, she told me that she felt my heart chakra was blocked. There was some old stuck energy I still needed to clear.

"Do I have permission to ask your angels some questions?" Kamala asked me, obviously knowing how important it was to always get permission from a person before you performed any sort of healing on them.

"Yes, of course!" I replied, curious to see what she would ask.

"Does this block at Patty's heart chakra have to do with her hurt from her ex-husband in this lifetime?" she asked my angels. "Not all of it, your angels replied," she relayed to me.

"Does this block at Patty's heart have to do with something Patty is aware of?" she asked my angels again. "Yes, you are aware of it, your angels replied," Kamala said.

"Does this block at Patty's heart have to do with something in this lifetime?" She asked for more clarity. "Not all of it, your angels replied."

"Does this block have to do with issues from another lifetime?" Kamala asked. "The answer is yes, and so we will proceed with the healing for your actions in your past life."

"Now I would like you to close your eyes. Start taking slow, deep breaths. We are going to call to you, your self as the abusive man in your past life, to come forward now," Kamala gently instructed me.

I closed my eyes. I started to breathe slow and deep. I was a little apprehensive because I was still so ashamed of myself and my behavior. But I was eager to do the healing as I was anxious to apologize and ask forgiveness of my wife. Kamala led me through a meditation that allowed me to clear my mind and center inward. Immediately, it began....

Suddenly, the front walk of a house comes into view. It is a small property and close in proximity to others. The front walk runs perpendicular to the house, leading directly to the sidewalk and the street. Neatly-trimmed grass was on each side of the walk. At the edge of property, running along the sidewalk, is a short white picket fence.

Standing with his feet firmly planted on the wooden boards that comprised the floor of the front porch is a man. Straight and rigid, he stands, his tenseness palpable. I could see the back of his head: short black hair, thick and wavy but neatly combed, peeks out from below the rim of his black hat. Dressed all in black, he seems very ordinary. Looking through his eyes, I realize it is I in my former life.

"I see a front walk leading to the street," I tell Kamala, filled with trepidation at what may happen next. "Wait. I see a figure, a woman on the sidewalk."

The woman is standing directly in front of me at the end of the walk.

"It's my wife!" I cry out, recognizing her as the cowering figure from my regression.

"My wife is stooped over still," I say, starting to cry—pained by her stooped shoulders and downward gaze.

"She is still weak and beaten down. She seems so sad," I go on, heartbroken at the obvious pain my wife is still in.

"Look at her and tell her you're sorry," Kamala gently nudges me.

"I'm sorry. I'm so sorry!" I cry out. "I never meant to hurt you!"

My wife looks up at me, silent in her response.

"I didn't understand what I was doing!" I choke the words out, openly crying now. The pain from my actions is overwhelming. "It wasn't your fault!" I cry.

My words are starting to permeate the deep pain blanketing my wife, and she starts to slowly straighten up.

"It wasn't your fault. It wasn't you," I continue on, sending her all the love that I can—trying to help, to erase the pain that my misguided actions caused. "I am so sorry!"

Several moments pass. Each plea for forgiveness reaches deeper, closer to her heart. The cowering figure in front of me begins to slowly rise up, unfolding like a flower bud opening up to face the sun. It is truly one of the most beautiful things I have ever seen.

She is not bent over anymore. My wife is standing straight, and she is looking directly at me.

"She is standing tall!" I exclaim, sobbing now. "Her body is straight, and she is holding her head high."

My wife has received a healing. She has accepted my request for forgiveness, and the pain and the hurt seem to have left her.

"I love you! I love you so much!" My heart breaks open, and unconditional love pours out.

A white light emanates from her. She is radiant in her joy! I watch her from my position on the front porch, grateful for the opportunity to apologize. She stands strong before me, and I know that the healing is hers to fully receive.

Wanting to embrace her but sensitive to the fact that she may not want physical contact with me, I am overjoyed as she starts to walk toward me. I run to meet her and stand before her, waiting for her cue. As she holds out her arms to me, I look into her eyes and see genuine love shining back at me. I now know she has truly forgiven me, and I melt into her arms, embracing her fully.

All too soon, my wife turns to walk away. I watch her as she walks along the sidewalk, her back straight and her head held high. In a moment, when she reaches the edge of the fence, she will be gone.

"I love you!" I shout to her once again. "Thank you for forgiving me!"

Stopping at the edge of the fence, she turns to look at me one last time.

"I love you too," she says with a relaxed grin, the kind that is shared only between the closest of friends. And with that, she is gone.

As tears stream down my face, I wrap my arms tightly around myself. Unable to integrate the overwhelming emotions I am feeling, I am hoping that if I squeeze hard enough, they will somehow be released. The knowledge that my wife is no longer hurting overflows within me. I am filled with gratitude for the gift I have just received, the knowledge that another is no longer in pain.

Kamala gives me a few minutes to process what just happened, and then she starts to speak again.

"It is now time for you to forgive yourself," she reminds me.

I feel a sudden jolt, a sickness in my stomach. "No, I don't think I can do that." I weep.

It is one thing to apologize to another, but I was still ashamed of my actions. How could I forgive myself for emotionally and physically abusing another?

"You must forgive yourself to heal," Kamala tells me. "You have to try."

I see myself. I am still standing on the front porch. I am stuck. Emotionally, I can't go further.

"I don't know what to do!" I cry.

"This is part of your Self, and your whole Self must be reintegrated back into you," Kamala goes on. "Picture yourself telling this part of you that you are forgiven."

I know I must try. I have come too far and done too much work to stop now. Using all of my strength, I will the figure in front of me to turn around and face me, knowing he is as reluctant as I am to come to terms with our actions.

Slowly, he turns around. Thin, with a slight build, his features are angular, harsh, really, his jet-black hair and mustache emphasizing the harshness. I am staring into dark eyes that are mine, eyes of a man that I am ashamed of.

How could I possibly forgive the part of me that hurt another so deeply? I am repulsed by it, stuck in my shame. I can't move forward.

"I can't do it! I can't feel love or forgiveness for this part of me!" I yell.

"This part of you has given you a gift, Patty," Kamala reminds me. *"This part of you was courageous enough to show up in that lifetime and experience the anger for you. This part of you lived through the anger and the bitterness and the loneliness so that you would be able to feel the opposite emotions. This part of you did that so that you could truly understand and experience love and complete acceptance now."*

I try to process what Kamala is saying. I do believe that we incarnate to have the physical experience and to feel emotions. I understand the duality of emotions. There is a spectrum, and on one end of the spectrum is love, and on the opposite end of the spectrum is fear. Each emotion on the spectrum has its opposite emotion. We can't truly understand one emotion until we experience its opposite.

"Thank this part of you for the gift you have been given." Kamala nudges me.

That makes it easier. I know we choose our experiences. This part of me chose to incarnate into the physical form and have that experience to further my soul development. It gets muddy for me here, though, because I also believe that with free will, our soul can get sidetracked or a little lost because of the choices we make. I believe this aspect of me got a little lost.

I am still sobbing, but I am determined. My heart has softened toward the man standing in front of me. I understand that he is a lost part of me that I need to forgive and welcome back. My Spirit needs to be whole again.

I begin to send healing white light to him, enveloping him in the radiance. As the light wraps around him, I try with all of my might to feel real love and forgiveness for this lost *part of me. I am acutely aware that my emotions need to be genuine or the healing won't take place.*

Slowly, I see him start to change from black to a dark brown. The Divine Light is healing him.

"I understand," I cry out. "I thank you for your gift."

He is changing further. He is a dark bronze color now.

"I forgive you, and I love you." I weep, overwhelmed, my emotions true.

He continues to lighten to a bronze and then gold. He is losing his physicality.

"It is OK. It is time to come back." I cry, cracking open the part of my heart I have kept closed.

All remnants of his physical form are now gone. He is becoming all light, a pure, white light.

I invite the light into me, welcoming home this lost aspect of myself. My breath catches, and my heart hammers in my chest as I accept the white light, allowing it to fully reintegrate into my Spirit.

"He is gone," I sob, rocking back and forth on the bed. "I am whole."

Drenched in tears, Kamala hands me tissues. She gives me a few minutes to collect myself before speaking.

"How do you feel?" she asks me very lovingly.

How do I feel? I feel grateful.

CHAPTER 13

Gratitude, I found, could be complicated. So could faith. They were easy to feel when life moved along according to plan. But when life seemed to have a mind of its own, that's when they could get tricky.

Months had passed. The flowers had all bloomed, and the leaves had fallen from the trees, left as dark remnants of their former brilliance on the forest floor. The warmth of our beautiful sun, which has always strengthened and nurtured me, had cooled. Nature was prepared to rest.

I tried to feel the stillness. Relax and let the natural rhythm of our earth soothe my troubled mind. But as winter was almost upon us and the days were getting darker and drearier, I felt my confidence in my purpose and my work starting to waver. Instead of basking in the brilliance of my own inner light, I felt more and more like a dark remnant left on the forest floor.

Trying to strike a balance between working on deepening my own spiritual understanding and promoting and sharing the messages in my first book, I realized, with much humility, that both were much more difficult than I had anticipated.

To make matters worse, what I considered to be my complete leap of faith, and allowance of the Divine to guide me, was actually less of a leap than I thought.

I found myself attached to what I thought following my Divine life purpose was supposed to look like. I realized that although I thought I was going to allow the Divine to guide me, I still had some definite control issues. I had already mapped out in my head what I believed was going to happen. In reality, my ideas were very different from what was happening.

I was also waiting for Divine clarity, inspiration to start writing my second book. From the beginning of my journey, I had been receiving messages that I was not only to write a book, but I was to write a series of books. My first book was truly Divinely written, as I was shown specifically what to write. My second book, I only knew, was to be on angels, but I didn't know what I was supposed to say.

How is this happening? and *Did I misunderstand my purpose?* or *What am I doing wrong?* were thoughts frequently running through my head.

I felt vulnerable. My confidence had started to deteriorate, and I doubted what I knew in my heart. I searched for a kernel of truth, something that I could hold on to.

I chose this dance, I kept reminding myself. *My experiences are not random or coincidental. There is a definite plan in place, and living my life's purpose matters.*

If I believed that, then I had to believe that everything was fine and happening according to the Divine Plan and Divine timing. But that's a hard nut to crack when days, weeks, and months go by without seeing real progress.

I needed a break. I was too much in my own head, and I was starting to lose perspective. I contacted my friend Barbara Slaine to see if she could meet for lunch. Barbara runs a wellness center and was also walking her spiritual path. She had inspired me for some time, and I appreciated both her great insight and her lighthearted way.

We met the next week at a vegetarian restaurant that Barbara had recommended. Over salads and green tea, we caught up and shared what had been happening, or, more correctly, what I thought was not happening for me.

Toward the end of our lunch, Barbara said, "You know I'm the 'Queen of Canceling,' and I almost canceled today. In fact, I had to rearrange my schedule to have lunch with you today, but something was telling me to come. Now I understand why."

I was intrigued. Barbara had obviously received Divine clarity; I loved when that happened.

"I have an amazing energy worker and healer staying at my center now. She works with energies beyond the fourth dimension to help people clear and release any blocks that are inhibiting their ability to hear Source," Barbara explained. "I think you should see her. Her name is Mearah Marqua."

I have learned to follow guidance when it is presented to me, and I knew that Barbara telling me about Mearah was not coincidental. Following my heart, I called Mearah the next day and made an appointment to see her the next week. I wasn't sure what to expect, but Barbara's glowing recommendation was enough for me.

I arrived at the center the next week and was met by Mearah, a woman with long reddish-brown hair, a warm smile, and a humble demeanor. After exchanging pleasantries, Mearah explained a little of what would happen. She explained that she is a multidimensional healer and uses different modalities—sound, movement, clairvoyance, and assistance from spiritual guides—to clear and open energy pathways in our bodies. We would talk briefly; then I would lie on the table, and she would perform the energy work.

Mearah asked me why I had come to see her. What was I trying to achieve? I explained simply that I was walking my spiritual path and trying to deepen my spiritual connection to my Self and my guides, and I was feeling blocked. I wasn't making the progress I had hoped to make. What Mearah said next not only surprised me but, I believe, was a direct message from my guides.

"Are you an artist of some kind? Do you do something creative?" she asked me.

"No," I replied, not understanding the scope of her question.

"I see that you are to write a book, a series of books, really," she went on.

"Has Barbara told you about me?" I asked, wanting to see if Mearah knew I was an author.

"No, I haven't talked to Barbara about you. Why?" Mearah replied.

"Well, I have written a book, and I believe I am to write another one, but I am waiting for guidance on what to write," I explained.

"You will receive guidance on what to write, clarity from your guides," she said. "It will come. Wait."

I felt buoyed by her words. I knew in my heart that I was to write the book series, and I was waiting for clarity. But I was surprised again by her next words.

"Have you considered speaking? I see that your messages, your transmissions, are through your words, your written and spoken words."

"Yes!" I exclaimed. "I love to speak, and I have been doing many radio interviews, sharing the messages from my first book."

What I didn't tell her was that I felt in my heart that I was to speak to millions of people. My life and spiritual experiences so far had prepared me for this. My messages of healing and Oneness were a Universal Truth that needed to be heard.

"Your transmissions will be much larger than this. This is the beginning for you," she clarified. "I see you in front of many, many people. Your words, both written and spoken, are your healing transmissions and will help millions of people."

I was excited. After undergoing such uncertainty over the past few months, hearing Mearah's words gave me renewed faith and hope. She was telling me not only what I believed in my heart but what other healers had told me since the beginning of my journey. My belief in my life's purpose was reaffirmed. I silently thanked my angels and guides for sharing their words through Mearah.

I lay down on her massage table, and the next hour was spent with Mearah clearing the energetic pathways in my body so that I would be open to receiving Divine communication and guidance. She also explained that behind our heart center is a special activation point, emerald green in color, which is the gateway to our soul.

Suddenly feeling very drowsy, I dozed off during the activation and clearing. Afterward, Mearah explained that it was not unusual that I did so, as people experience and respond to energy in many different ways. She handed me a glass of water and asked me how I was feeling.

"Great!" I said. "I'm not exactly sure what you did, but I feel lighter, somehow refreshed."

CHAPTER 14

"Clarity on what to write will come. Wait," Mearah had said.

I trusted what Mearah had told me, but being patient and sitting idly by, however, are two very different things. While I was trying to learn to have more patience and allow the Divine energies and my guides to lead me, I knew I needed to keep learning. Developing a regular spiritual practice was the key to maintaining my focus. Each day, I spent time reading or meditating or engaged in spiritual practice that helped me go inward and invite connection.

Recently, I had been doing a series of sound meditations. I had found that listening to either music, or other types of sound recordings, during my meditations helped me to focus and stay present in the meditation. On this particular day, I was listening to a sound recording for a heart-chakra meditation. The recommendation was to be still and either to listen to the sounds and feel the vibrations resonate through your heart center or visualize a miniature of yourself in your heart center and send yourself love.

I decided I was going to settle in and just allow the sounds to reverberate through my heart center. I thought it would be really interesting to actually feel the vibrations in my body, and as I had done so much work surrounding my heart chakra, I assumed there was nothing more to heal. But as with most things in my life at that time, my plans gave way to a higher intention.

No sooner had I put my headphones on and closed my eyes than the vision began. Immediately, I saw a miniature of myself in my heart center.

This is odd, I thought, since my intention was to relax and feel the music move through my heart center.

Well, if I am to see an image of myself, I am going to have her stand with her arms outstretched with joy, I thought, ready to fully move past the hurt I had experienced in the past couple of years.

However, the vision continued on its own, like my previous experiences had. I was simply a witness to the experience, similar to watching a movie playing on a screen.

In my mind's eye, I see myself in my heart center, and I try to envision myself standing up with my arms outstretched wide, owning my power and feeling great joy. But I couldn't. The image of me is one of my being suddenly and very forcefully squatting down, with my head down and my arms wrapped tight around my knees.

What is going on?

I try to stand her up, sending my energy, my will, to her. As hard as I try, I can't budge her, this image of myself. She remains squatting down as low as the ground, forming a tight ball with her arms wrapped around her knees and her head down.

What in the world could be happening? *I thought, again looking for some understanding.*

"You were abused in a former life," *I clearly heard, and I instantly knew that my Higher Self was speaking.*

What? Abused?

Though shaken, I immediately know in my heart that the details of the abuse don't matter. I have learned enough to know that what had happened to me in a past physical form had nothing to do with my true spiritual Self. This knowledge allowed me to open my heart and act without judgment. What was important was that I healed the aspect of myself that was showing itself to me now. The aspect that was so traumatized and filled with shame that it couldn't lift its head up or unwrap its arms from its legs.

"It's OK", *I silently tell this aspect of myself.* "I know it was not you. I know it was not your fault."

I feel such a rush of love toward this part of myself, this vulnerable and hurting aspect of me, that I want to wrap her in my arms and hold her tight. Not being able to physically do so, I envelop her with white healing light.

"You have nothing to be ashamed of. What happened to you in your physical form does not affect your true nature," *I lovingly tell her.*

The light is swirling around her, wrapping her, permeating every cell of her. Gradually, the white light starts to turn a golden hue. I am surprised because I did not send her a golden light, but my surprise lasts only for an instant. I have started to see the golden light more and more frequently in my everyday life, and I am beginning to come to the realization that it is also an aspect of me.

"It is time to heal," *I offer my words to her.* "It is time."

I direct all of my energy and love to the image of myself. Slowly, my body starts to unfold. My head rises up from my knees, and my arms release their tight grip on my legs. As the golden light continues to mend my broken Spirit, I tentatively start to stand up—gingerly, at first—unsure if it is safe. Slowly, my trust deepens, and it feels good, like a deep stretch feels to tight muscles.

Swathed in the radiance of the golden light, I lovingly remind myself that all is well. She is well. She is whole. She has nothing to be ashamed of. As I continue to speak, her presence becomes more powerful. With her arms reaching high above her, and her legs spread to create a secure base below her, her shame is released, and she feels her wholeness. Her healing is complete.

I cry tears of joy, and I am ready to integrate and welcome her back into my full Self.

"I love you! It is OK now," I tell her as her light and her form effortlessly merge into mine.

Stunned, I take a deep breath and sit for a moment, processing what has happened. Thinking that the meditation is over, I am ready to open my eyes . . . when I am startled to see the shell or outline of a male figure crouching down in front of me. His form is similar to a runner poised in position before a race, his fingertips lightly touching the ground, but his head is lowered in sadness.

I realize that this is another aspect of me that needs healing. This aspect seems to be filled with a deep sadness. However, since I only see his outline, I believe that I have already done much of his work, but until all aspects are fully reintegrated, there is more work to be done.

Instinctively, I know what to do, and I begin to send him healing light, the light enveloping and swirling around and through him. This light is a golden hue, and it fills every broken or lost aspect of him, replacing the sadness with a great love.

Slowly, he begins to stand. His head lifts up, and his fingers release the ground they were resting on. His long, strong legs start to straighten as his upper body unfolds. It is as if the sadness had been weighing him down, and now, with the sadness leaving his body, there is lightness to him. The release is welcome and long overdue. He, as an aspect of me, is standing, arms outstretched, glowing with the golden light.

I stand before him as a golden female figure. I welcome and accept him into my heart. Gratefully, I watch as he steps into me, returning to me another lost aspect of myself.

I feel amazing. Grateful, powerful, and humbled are just a few of the emotions running through me.

Suddenly and unexpectedly, I am confused. The image of my Self is now unclear. A moment ago, I had clearly seen myself as a golden female figure. Now that I had just integrated a part of myself that was a male form, I couldn't clearly see myself.

Was I a female figure? Was I a male figure? Was I genderless? *My mind tries to put form to my Spirit.*

My Spirit, my Higher Self, answers me with a beautiful vision. My confused, unclear presence starts to release all aspects of a human form. I see myself transform from a physical body infused with golden light to only golden Light.

Golden beings surround my Higher Self. My Higher Self as the golden light becomes a golden being too. I understand. I am being shown that I am also a golden being. That is my true Self.

"I am one also, a golden being?" *I ask for confirmation.*

"Yes, you are," *I am told.*

My body feels different. I feel wholeness, an expansion, but also a beautiful sense of peace inside of me.

"I am Light, and that is my true Self." *I innately understand; a sense of clarity fills my being.* "I limit myself when

I see only from my human perspective."

    I sit with this revelation. Breathing deeply, I am eventually able to slow my crying until just a few tears of gratitude are left on my cheeks.

CHAPTER 15

"The water dragon," I exclaimed. "You have got to be kidding me! I can't write a blog on the water dragon."

I was confused because I had set my intention that the animal-totem card that I pulled would be the correct message for that week's *Messages from the Animals* blog post.

Messages from the Animals, my weekly blog, was a continuation of my first book in the sense of bringing awareness to the Oneness we share with our Self, each other, and the natural world. The animals, acting as totems, are our messengers and our guides. I wrote my blog, retelling my personal experiences with the animals and the messages and guidance given to me. If an animal has not shown up for me lately, I will pull an animal totem card from one of my animal oracle decks and write about the symbolism of that animal.

I put the deck away. I felt a little unsettled because I knew that I had pulled the card with the intention that it had a message to be shared, and messages from the Divine are never wrong. I knew I could trust what came forward for me. However, I still did not feel that I should write my blog on the water dragon. The rest of the day was uneventful. I busied myself with other work and decided to wait until the next day to pull another card from my deck.

After having my coffee the next morning, I settled down at my desk. Taking the deck of animal totem cards out once again, I began to shuffle. The deck has a little over thirty cards in it, and I wanted to make sure I shuffled it well. I breathed deep and set my intention again that the card that I pulled would be a message to be shared. I shuffled the cards until I felt it was time to stop. I turned over the top card.

It was the water dragon.

Oh no! There has to be a mistake. I cannot write a blog on a water dragon. People are not ready for dragons yet!

Needing time to think about it, I put the deck down and got up to get another cup of coffee. The water dragon definitely had significance, or I would not have pulled it two days in a row. But I didn't feel that it was the right animal to write about in my blog. Most people were just opening up to the idea of animal totems; I definitely didn't think a blog on the water dragon would be well received.

With my second cup of steaming-hot coffee nestled in my hands, I settled back at my desk. I decided I should research animal totems and dragons together and see what came up. Maybe there was an animal closely related to dragons that I could use. My search came up with the Komodo dragon. Not wanting to give up on the water dragon's message, I looked closer at the Komodo dragon. As hard as I tried, it just didn't feel right to me. To me, the Komodo dragon really was just a giant lizard, not a dragon at all!

I was perplexed. The water dragon had to have a message to share, considering it came up two days in a row. I decided to look up the water dragon's symbolism. Maybe that would give me a clue.

The message of the water dragon is that *forgotten or repressed memories in the unconscious mind are now emerging into the conscious mind. Confronting any negativity these memories bring up with love and compassion will bring a greater peace to your soul and a connection to all life. Integrating these emotions back into your soul will bring balance and wholeness.*

I almost laughed out loud. The message of the water dragon was meant for me!

I sat there for a long time with a big smile on my face. The Divine never ceased to amaze me. I have no doubt that the connection between our physical form and the spiritual realm is strong. There are loving and supportive beings all around us. But I am still impressed with how creative they are in communicating with us!

I knew the message of the water dragon was connected to the heart-chakra meditation and healing I did the day before. It was confirmation that what I had experienced in my meditation was real and powerful. What I didn't realize was that there was still more information to come.

CHAPTER 16

As things always seem to come in threes, the next day was one I had been anticipating for a while. My friend Barbara was hosting a very special guest: Eve Kerwin, a channel for White Buffalo Woman, who was an important spiritual figure for the Lakota Indian tribe. At the time, I did not know much about White Buffalo Woman, but it is believed that she is either the reincarnation of, or the same archetypal energy as, the Egyptian god Isis, Mary, the mother of Jesus, Eve, the original mother figure in the Christian tradition, and Kwan Yin, a Hindu goddess who is also representative of the energies of the Divine Mother. Feeling a strong connection with all the entities, I was excited to meet a person that channeled such immense energy.

I didn't know what to expect from the evening. Being conscious to keep my spiritual experiences as organic as possible, I have always purposely done very little research before attending different events or workshops. This was no different. I was content to just show up and let Spirit guide the evening, and I would have been happy to simply meet the channel. However, I was delighted to find out it was going to be much, much more.

Arriving, I warmly greeted Barbara and took my seat in the semicircle of chairs that encircled Eve. Looking around, I saw about twenty people, both men and women, of various ages and sizes and shapes, waiting with anticipation for the evening ahead. They looked like my family and friends, like people I would meet at the grocery store or on the soccer field watching their kids play. I wondered about them, my fellow participants. *Why were they here? What has their spiritual journey been like?* and *What has led them here this evening?* People just like me that were yearning to know more, to feel more connected with their Higher Power. I smiled and took a deep breath, feeling right at home.

Eve began the evening by explaining a little about herself, her life experiences, including her spiritual awakening and how she became a channel for White Buffalo Woman. Her demeanor was very friendly and approachable, and she soon had everyone feeling at ease. To my delight, she then explained that each one of us would receive a channeled message that evening.

The message would be channeled through White Buffalo Woman, but very likely, another aspect of the Divine would show up to deliver the message. Our soul would call forward whatever message we were supposed to hear. It could be from our Higher Self, an archangel, or other ascended masters such as Jesus or St. Germaine. White Buffalo Woman would also clear our energetic fields and remove any past connections to energies that were holding us back or preventing us from living our highest and greatest good.

Spirit was truly guiding the evening, and we would receive our messages in the order that White Buffalo Woman called us. In the dim light that shone from the candles, White Buffalo Woman would settle her penetrating gaze on someone and extend her pointed finger to call them forward.

The room was silent with anticipation. Eve went into her trance, and White Buffalo Woman entered into her. I listened intently as each person was called up. Energetic ties and cords were cut that held people to energies that no longer served them. A cord was cut from a dead twin that died in the mother's womb. Another from a family member that was lost. Still more ties were cut that held people to past lives.

Archangel Michael, St. Germaine, and others showed up with messages. Many messages were also from the person's own Higher Self. Past lives were revealed. Places on this earth, such as Bali and Peru, were mentioned as places that certain people needed to visit to reclaim pieces of their hearts in this life. Soul mates and soul paths were discussed.

It was incredible to listen to each person's experience and how much the messages resonated with them. Soon, White Buffalo Woman's gaze fell on me, and with her finger pointed toward me, I was called forward. Excitedly, I stood up, fumbled with my phone to turn on the recording device, and approached her. Standing directly in front of her, I stared into her eyes. I looked for some recognition from her, something in her gaze that I could connect to. What I found was a void, a spacious, peaceful and deep void. Eve was not present, but White Buffalo Woman certainly was. She seemed to look through me, her gaze at once penetrating and vacant. My body tingled with anticipation of the message I would receive.

Eve, as White Buffalo Woman, spoke in a rhythmic staccato-like cadence. Her voice and demeanor completely transformed from earlier that evening. Below is a direct transcription of the recording of my experience:

"I am your Higher Self calling. It is time for you to take a deeper look inside. It is time for you to truly begin to reside through the center of your own Divine heart. Your heart center is begging for attention from you. You see deep, deep down inside of thee; it seems that you tend to forget about you personally.

"Day after day, through your everyday living way, you truly give, give, give, but you need to now give more to you. You are forgetting yourself through your own neglectful way. We will now explain why this tends to be for you. Three lifetimes before this present one, you, dearest one, were totally overcome through fear. This was a lifetime for you that truly plagued your mind's way of thinking. You were completely afraid of your spouse. And within that lifetime, we say your spouse would in one way or another, threaten you day after day. You feared his physical presence around you. His presence tormented you literally.

"You were the same age within your physical body today as when your spouse passed away rather suddenly. You felt such a relief. You felt free. However, as the days progressed, the freedom began to turn to guilt. Deep guilt. You felt that you were insensitive, and you turned yourself against you. The fear continued to plague your body for the rest of that lifetime.

"Presently, your soul wishes to say to you today through your own heartfelt way, 'I have made progress as a woman, especially for myself today, in this lifetime.' You see, this lifetime is all about gathering all of the thoughts and emotions and feelings, not only from this lifetime but of course, if you could remember, from your past. But you are here to give yourself one final energetic blast and to basically *absolve yourself through your own feminine way and make peace with yourself through your own heart through your own deepest way that you are OK.*

"So this is a throwback effect that you continued to work through, that your soul did elect to wrap up that karma from three lifetimes ago in conjunction with your lifetime today. So we say hip hip hooray and enjoy your life day after day. See yourself, feel yourself, know yourself differently. Do you wish to question?"

"Will I be meeting my soul mate in this lifetime?" I asked.

"We will say quite possibly. The reason we say quite possibly is because this is part of your destiny. Yes, it will be up to you, the way in which you will follow through with you in regard to your outlook, your feelings day after day. You are destined to attract this to come toward you absolutely—this is part of your destiny, but it is up to thee if you will allow this to be.

So we are tipping you off. Free feel; finally feel free! Clear? Peace."

It was over. I was grateful because I received validation from my Higher Self that the vision and information I received in the message of the water dragon and during my heart meditation were correct. I was most definitely deepening my spiritual understanding and connection.

But I was also disappointed. After listening to some of the others' experiences, I wanted my Higher Self to tell me to go to Bali, or some other exotic place, and find my soul mate. Something that was more interesting and cool than telling me I am not joyful enough yet. To hear that I am still neglecting my heart was a little hard to take. For the past four years, all I had been doing was working on healing my heart. Seriously, how much more was there to do?

But I think I just got permission to have some real fun. Maybe I would take a trip to Bali . . . .

CHAPTER 17

The bitter, dark winter days of January had me firmly in their grip. It was one of the coldest and dreariest winters in recent history, and there was no end in sight. Day after day, I sat alone at my desk. I breathed. I meditated. I immersed myself in my work and engrossed myself in my interfaith seminary studies. But it was still difficult for me.

The obligations of everyday life were becoming more and more evident. My head was telling me that with two children to support and college to pay for, I needed to move forward and start earning a decent living again. Deep doubts crept in during the silent moments, and stress reared its ugly head when I looked at my bank statement.

My heart, on the other hand, could not begin to imagine doing anything other than continuing on my spiritual path. Every fiber of my being knew that I was where I was supposed to be, and my life purpose was to be of spiritual service. The thought of doing anything else made my body physically ache. I had to remind myself more and more frequently that I was fully supported and loved by my spiritual teachers and guides, and my worries were of the personality, my ego. My Spirit was stronger, and I could, and I would, manifest an increased abundance in my life.

With prayer and invitation, Spirit filled me and sustained me, and I continued my practice and my work. My focus was on spreading the messages of Oneness and connection to ourselves, each other, and all living beings. However, I was still impatient to start writing my second book.

What could my story be? What do I have to offer that hasn't been offered before?

Then, as Divine intervention always works perfectly and without warning, I received my answer. It was so simple and so clear that I was surprised I hadn't seen it before. It was right before me the whole time.

A few months prior, I had started writing articles for different spiritual magazines. My writing allowed me the opportunity to be of service and share spiritual messages. It was nearing the end of the month when I remembered that I had been asked a few weeks earlier if I could write an article on angels. As I had no idea what to write, the request had rolled around in my head, formless. Not wanting to disappoint the magazine editor, I forced myself to put pen to paper and try to come up with some ideas. At that time, I wrote articles based on my personal experiences, so to get started, I jotted down some experiences that I had been having: meditations, healings, astral travel, past-life regressions . . . the list went on. Smiling, I looked at the list and shook my head in amazement and gratitude for the gifts I had been given.

I would love to write about all of this, but it is not on angels, and it would be a very long article! Feeling amused, I looked at my list again. *Wait a minute . . . the golden beings . . . . They are my angels.*

Immediately, I thought of the first regression with Maria when I saw the golden angel holding the sword. I had forgotten he was an angel. Since then, I saw and thought of them as golden beings. How did I not remember they were angels?

Excited, I realized that I didn't have one article here but a series of articles. I started to outline my thoughts, when real clarity finally set in. This was not a series of blog articles . . . . This was my second book!

I was anxious to start writing, but I didn't feel quite ready yet. Mearah came to mind. Mearah, the energy healer that I had visited a couple of months prior. I felt that it was time to go back, to receive more help in clearing whatever residual or stuck energy was still holding me back.

I made an appointment to see her the next week. Immediately, my being felt lighter, and I was filled with gratitude for the people and help that I had all around me.

The day of the appointment came quickly, and I consciously centered my thoughts and feelings during the long drive to my appointment. Despite my insecurities, I knew I had made much progress, but I was still anxious to hear what insights Mearah would share.

Opening the large wooden door at the center, Mearah greeted me. Dressed in a colorful top with beautiful hues of light greens and purples, she looked well. I was taken aback at how happy I was to see her. I felt like I was visiting an old friend.

Settled in comfortably on her couch, we chatted for a few minutes. I explained that I had been working hard at deepening my spiritual understanding and connection, and I was hoping to clear any stuck or negative energy that might still be lingering and holding me back. Mearah surprised me by mentioning that she sees more of a golden light around me, and buoyed by her statement, I asked if I could record the session so I wouldn't forget any of the messages.

"*Of course,*" she replied. "*There is clarity here. You have a knowing, a direct knowing and that is one of the ways that you navigate. There is a lot going on around you energetically. It's like all the players are coming into position. The golden lights and your whole system are getting calibrated to release any resistance and receive more.*

"*You are safe and being Divinely guided. The gold, the angels, and there is also a sphere of consciousness around you, a collective. We might remove any residue of the pain from this or parallel lives, as there is a little and it is on the surface. We will bring it forward to transmute, as everything is vibration.*

"*Please lie down on the table and focus on a double triangle star within the center of your head. The pineal, pituitary, and hypothalamus glands form the triangle.*"

I lay down on the table. Mearah asks me to get comfortable, close my eyes, and take nice deep breaths in through my nose and out through my mouth. Mearah starts to speak:

"*Moving into receiving. Look up behind closed lids, and pull the light in from the center of your head, and exhale it down through your spine. Good, and then relax your eyes and continue to bring the light in. As the light comes in, it opens up your brain center and your neuro passageways. Think about it activating the pineal, pituitary and hypothalamus glands with the thought of a double triangle in the center of the head. It is about two inches round, a six-sided star. It might be moving or it might be still. It also might be more than one triangle, symbolizing more dimensions opening up in there too.*"

Mearah works for some time, clearing and opening the energy fields in my body, and then begins to channel one of her spiritual guides. Her voice—the tone and cadence have shifted to a deeper, more commanding and loving tone.

"Dear Patty, it is important for you to continue to do as you are doing . . . .

"And you are completely protected on this journey, for indeed this is your souls' purpose. The alignment of who you are coming forward in this time to communicate, to bring the magic back to the world. To allow others to remember their magic, their ability to connect in many, multidimensional ways, and there is great love that surrounds you, a great love that emanates through you. Continue to trust and allow these energies to move through you."

Mearah starts breathing differently, and the channeling ends. She speaks.

"So now take some nice deep breaths. The energy is going to keep moving with you, as you know that this will integrate more. Get a sense of the bottoms of your feet. Put your focus there, and help to bring the energy in. Focus at the center of your head, and focus in the navel area. There is also a golden disc there at the navel; it is an activation point. The golden light continues to flood in through all of your organs, strengthening, centering, and grounding the frequency."

More minutes passed as I focused on the energetic work that Mearah explained. She then handed me a glass of water and spoke again.

"This is really great. You are really integrating the energies in a nice flow. It's like a celebration because you have chosen to trust and are open to receive."

"I feel so grateful for the experiences and the messages I am given," I shared. "I just keep showing up, knowing that even on the days when doubts try to creep in that, as a spiritual being, I am supported and loved and all is as it should be."

"You are supported," Mearah said as she smiled. "There is an orchestration around you, and this is something that you came to do."

As I hugged Mearah, a deep knowing filled my being, and I understood. *We are the orchestrators of our own dance. Our thoughts, emotions, and actions creating the very movements we dance to. The energy is increasing; the vibration is rising,* and as Mearah said, *"The players are coming into position; they are stepping onto the stage."*

Driving home, I turned on the car radio. A song by Pink was playing. Smiling, I turned up the volume, and as I started to sing, a realization came over me. *It is time to dance. I have surrendered to the dance, my dance.*

Your dance is waiting to begin.

VALUABLE RESOURCES FOR YOUR JOURNEY

Marie Marchesseault, traditional Usui and Rainbow Reiki master teacher www.reidirejuvenation.massageplanet.com

Rev. Kamala Snow, OUnI interspiritual counselor/minister, soul coach kamalasnow13@gmail.com

Maria C. Castillo, L.C.S.W, psychotherapist and hypnotherapist www.lifebetweenlivestherapy.com/

Rev. Lynette Turner, Positivoligist™ www.positivebliss.co

Barbara Slaine, The LipheBalance Center www.liphebalance.com

Eve Kerwin, shamanic healer and channel www.evekerwinwhitebuffalowoman.com

Lori Ann Spagna, speaker, luminary, visionary, and best-selling author www.lorispagna.com

Jeffrey Chappell, international best-selling author
www.answersfromsilence.com

Kate Large, best-selling author, founder of Soul Kisses Spiritual Whispers and The Game of Life Mastery
www.soulkisses.com

Christine Guerrera, LMFT PsychoSpiritual coaching and therapy
www.insightswellnesscenter.com/

Chris Mentch, singer/songwriter and poet
www.cmentch.com

ABOUT THE AUTHOR

Rev. Patricia Brooks is a sacred storyteller and an ordained interfaith minister. Her life's purpose is to help others by sharing her sacred story and the sacred stories of others. Rev. Patricia understands the beauty and power in our stories and how in sharing our stories we connect to the Collective Consciousness, our Oneness.

Rev. Patricia shares her sacred story through her book series *God is in the Little Things*. Her first book *Messages from the Animals* and her current book *Messages from the Golden Angels* are Divinely guided and are the honest and raw retelling of her true spiritual experiences as she walks her spiritual path.

Join Rev. Patricia on her tele-summit series **Sacred Stories** as she brings the sacred stories and spiritual abilities of the inspirational and cutting edge spiritual leaders of today to you!

http://www.sacredstoriestelesummit.com

Enjoy the powerful and compelling stories shared through **Sacred Stories Publishing**, Rev. Patricia's book and marketing company whose mission is to Bring the Voices of Divine Light to the World.

http://www.sacredstoriespublishing.com

Throughout life Rev. Patricia has earned her Bachelors of Science in Business Administration, her Masters of Arts in Education, and she is ordained from One Spirit Interfaith Seminary.

Rev. Patricia worked in the corporate and educational worlds for many years and proudly served six years as a sergeant in the U.S. Marine Corps.

On a more personal note she is a proud mom of two daughters, an obsessive coffee drinker—Rev. Patricia drinks it black like any good former Marine does, and is the best friend of her little dog, Bear.

Learn more at www.revpatriciabrooks.com

www.ingramcontent.com/pod-product-compliance
Lightning Source LLC
Chambersburg PA
CBHW021152080526
44588CB00008B/306